101 Easy-to-Do Magic Tricks

by Bill Tarr

Illustrated by Frank Daniel

Dover Publications, Inc.
New York

Some of the tricks in this book involve the use of matches and other potentially hazardous items. Care should be taken when practicing or performing these tricks; adult supervision is advised for young children.

Published in Canada by General Publishing Company, Ltd., 30 Lesmill Road, Don Mills, Toronto, Ontario.
Published in the United Kingdom by Constable and Company, Ltd., 3 The Lanchesters, 162–164 Fulham Palace Road, London W6 9ER.

This Dover edition, first published in 1992, is an unabridged and updated republication of the work originally published under the title *101 Easy-to-Learn Classic Magic Tricks: Great, Super-Easy, No-Sleight-of-Hand Magic Tricks You Can Do with Everyday Objects* by Vintage Books, Random House, Inc., New York, in 1977.

Manufactured in the United States of America
Dover Publications, Inc., 31 East 2nd Street, Mineola, N.Y. 11501

Library of Congress Cataloging-in-Publication Data

Tarr, Bill, 1925–
    101 easy-to-do magic tricks / by Bill Tarr ; illustrated by Frank Daniel.
        p.   cm.
    Reprint. Originally published: 101 easy-to-learn classic magic tricks. New York : Vintage Books, 1977.
    Summary: A step-by-step guide to performing 101 magic tricks using easily available objects as props.
    ISBN 0-486-27367-9
    1. Conjuring—Juvenile literature. [1. Magic tricks.] I. Daniel, Frank, ill. II. Tarr, Bill, 1925–   101 easy-to-learn classic magic tricks. III. Title. IV. Title: One hundred one easy-to-do magic tricks. V. Title: One hundred and one easy-to-do magic tricks.
GV1548.T37   1992
793.8—dc20   92-22895
                                                                                      CIP
                                                                                      AC

To the handful of great
artists, past and present,
who have dedicated
themselves to magic, not
for fame and not for glory
but for the sheer love of
it, this book is humbly
dedicated . . . .

contents

preface

I have tried to fill this book with really good tricks that require neither sleight of hand nor anything in the way of apparatus that you can't assemble yourself. In that, I believe I have succeeded. All of the effects in this book can be made at home, with one exception—the Chinese Rings, which is such an important trick I couldn't resist including it even though it must be store-bought.

Some of these tricks are quite simple. Others are a bit involved, but virtually all of them are great magic—classic tricks like the Dollar Bill in the Lemon, the Rising Cards, the Chinese Rice Bowls and a great many more made famous by the great magicians of yesterday and today.

The stars next to each trick are there to guide you. The tricks marked with ★ are the easiest to prepare and present; the ★ ★ tricks are harder and consequently require more time and effort; and the ★ ★ ★ tricks are the hardest of all. None of them, however, are beyond your capabilities.

Remember, when you get involved in magic, you become a participant in an ancient and highly revered form of entertainment. You owe it to your fellow magicians to respect their art. Magic tricks are secrets that should never be revealed—not to friends, not to family, not to anyone! It spoils their fun and yours, and it violates a code of ethics that has survived for centuries.

If you are true to these ideals and you work hard to really perfect your tricks before you show them, you will be a welcome addition to the wonderful world of magic.

Good luck and have fun.

Sincerely,
Bill Tarr

introduction

questions and answers for the beginning magician

If this book is your introduction to magic, there are probably a great many questions you would like to have answered. In the next few pages I have tried to anticipate some of them.

Q. How did most magicians get started?

Most serious magicians seem to have acquired their addiction for magic at a very tender age, and in most instances it was a magical performance that furnished the inspiration. Great sleight-of-hand man Dai Vernon saw his first magician at the age of five and has been passionate about magic ever since. Card expert Cliff Green was a young teenager when he was inspired by the performances of Nate Leipzig and T. Nelson Downs, and by the time he was fifteen he had made up his mind to become a professional magician.

The incomparable Max Malini started at the age of fifteen, sparked by a local saloon-proprietor magician on New York's Bowery whom he used to watch perform; Harry Blackstone and Joseph Dunninger were inspired by Harry Kellar; and the list goes on and on. Even Robert Houdin, the first modern conjurer, tells how a street magician awakened him to the wonders of magic, and that was way back in 1823!

Glowing magazine ads were another source of inspiration. Fabulous coin manipulator Bobo tells how, at the age of thirteen, "The Unbreakable Match," price ten cents, and the catalog that accompanied it started him on the road to magic.

Q. I am a beginner. How should I get started?

Pick a simple trick from this book. Nothing elaborate or difficult to do or to make. Then learn it well. Do it in front of a mirror. Practice the words you are going to say and the motions you are going to make and keep practicing them over and over again until you are utterly certain you can do the trick to perfection. You don't want to fail, especially on your first trick. You need all the confidence you can muster, and the only way to get it is to practice your trick to the point where all the steps in it are as familiar to you as the letters in your name.

When you are certain that you have it down pat, show it to someone close to you. Do the trick, fool them with it, and thank them for watching, but don't under any circumstances repeat the trick or tell them how you do it. It spoils your fun and theirs.

When you can do your first trick well, go on to the next and perfect it. Never show anything to anybody until you are absolutely ready. There is nothing more disappointing to a beginner than flubbing a trick, and conversely, nothing more encouraging than doing it well.

Q. What trick should I learn first?

Ideally you should select an easy-to-do trick that you are sure you can master, and of course one that you will enjoy performing. Start with something simple and work your way up. When you make your choice, bear in mind that many of the tricks in this book are designed for use in an act and don't really make good single effects. Production tricks like the Drumhead Tube or the Inexhaustible Hat are not good by themselves, and of course they should never be done too close to or surrounded by your audience.

Your best bet is to start with one of the card tricks, perhaps Lazy Location (page 86) or Muscle Reading (page 88) or The Four Aces (page 80). Since they are self-working you can concentrate on your presentation, but don't take them for granted because they don't require dexterity. Practice them out loud in front of a mirror. They are superb tricks, but if you don't do them really well, you won't appreciate their full potential and neither will your audience.

Q. What are the basic branches of magic?

There are a number of magical specialties, but most magicians are familiar with all of them and dabble in most. Following are the broad general categories.

manipulation

Manipulative magicians specialize in tricks with coins, cards, balls, thimbles or other small objects which, by means of sleight of hand, they make appear, disappear, change color and perform other interesting gyrations. Manipulations generally require a great deal of skill and dexterity and usually take long hours of practice to perfect.

comedy

Comedy acts can range from magic presented with a light, humorous touch to the outrageous and uproarious comedy that magicians like The Great Ballantine perform, in which tricks that invariably go awry are merely the vehicles for the magician's antics.

mental

Mentalists specialize in magic of the mind—feats that appear to border on the supernatural or are within the realm of parapsychology. They predict future events, divine the past history of people they have never met, read minds, perform amazing experiments in ESP, drive automobiles while blindfolded, find hidden objects, and so on.

escape

Magicians like the late Harry Houdini and the very active Amazing Randi specialize in escaping from confines. They are handcuffed, shackled, roped and tied, nailed into boxes, straitjacketed and hung upside down from tall buildings, and so forth. Sometimes they are bolted or strapped into weird restraints, but they always manage to escape because they are magicians and escaping is their thing.

illusions

Magic on any scale is illusion, but the magicians who specialize in large tricks—sawing a woman in half, making elephants and lions disappear, floating beautiful girls through the air, and so on—are known as illusionists.

close-up

As the name implies, close-up magic is performed at close range and generally under very informal circumstances—at the dinner table, at bars, at social gatherings and so on. In recent years, close-up magic has become increasingly popular, and there are now a number of magicians who do set close-up acts or routines that they generally perform sitting down at a table. Tricks are frequently but not necessarily manipulative in nature—coins, cards, and so forth.

nightclub and stage

Magic performed onstage or in nightclubs can take any of the forms mentioned above, or it can consist of magic tricks of a general nature. The length of time the act takes varies with the situation and can run from an eight-minute theatre act to a full evening show performed at a high school auditorium.

Q. Should I specialize in a particular branch of magic?

At this point, chances are you shouldn't specialize in anything but good all-around magic. When you really have a feel for it— that is, when you have absorbed the basic principles of magic and can do a number of tricks of various types confidently and well—you may tend to lean in one direction or another. It's really all a process of natural selection.

It depends on your personal preferences, and they in turn are motivated by your abilities. If you are glib you'll find yourself performing tricks that give you an opportunity to speak. If you have a keen sense of humor, you may gravitate towards comedy magic. If cerebral activities intrigue you, you may end up doing mental magic. If you have a delicate touch and good coordination and you are stimulated by challenge, sleights with cards and coins may be your thing. If you are a dynamic, take-charge kind of person, who knows? You may end up like Howard Thurston, a master illusionist with dozens of assistants and tons of apparatus.

The ultimate direction your magic takes will depend on who you are and what you are, but for now that shouldn't be your concern. Your only real problem at the moment is to learn to do one trick superbly well. Select a trick, practice it to perfection, present it confidently and fool people with it. That's the first step and your biggest hurdle. The rest will come naturally, so don't worry about it now.

Q. Is magic an expensive hobby?

It all depends. There are top professionals whose only

expenditure for apparatus is the dollar or so it costs to buy a new deck of cards. On the other hand, full-sized stage illusions can cost thousands of dollars and top illusionists like the late Harry Blackstone carried dozens of them!

If you wanted to, you could accumulate a lot of apparatus. (Just to give you an idea, there are 648 pages in the Louis Tannen Inc. magic catalog!) It's fun to buy new effects, but from a really practical point of view it isn't at all necessary. A couple of good books to teach you technique, an occasional magazine to keep you abreast of what's going on, and a few good tricks are really all anyone needs.

Compared to photography, model railroading, radio-controlled models or, for that matter, stamp or coin collecting, magical expenditures are paltry, indeed. A book like Bobo's *Modern Coin Magic* costs around twenty dollars, but it has enough good material in it to keep you happily occupied for the next ten years.*

Q. What is the one most important rule in magic?

Practice.

Practice is the key to good magic. There is just no way around it. There is no way in the world you can achieve the smoothness and the confidence you need to present a trick well except by standing in front of your mirror and practicing diligently and intelligently.

Set yourself up properly and observe your actions with a critical eye. Don't repeat yourself mindlessly over and over again. Pay attention to what you are doing and make a conscious effort to improve—and you will!

Q. Do I have to practice a lot?

Although the tricks in this book require no sleight of hand, that doesn't mean that they don't require practice! *Every* trick does. I doubt if there is a trick in the world, no matter how mechanical and push-button it may be, that doesn't require some degree of practice.

At the very least, you have to familiarize yourself with your apparatus. You have to decide what you are going to say, and usually you have to work out a routine.

Remember, too, that no matter how familiar you are with the

*Reprinted by Dover in 1982 for significantly less!

effect you are working on, and no matter how smoothly it goes during practice, chances are that unless you are really an old pro, you won't be quite as cool in front of your audience as you are in front of your mirror.

Practice is what it's really all about. There isn't a skill in the world that occurs naturally. Hitting a ball, playing an instrument, singing a song, or writing your name all take practice and lots of it, and that goes double for magic!

Q. Is sleight of hand difficult to learn?

Not really. There are moves that are very difficult and involved, but you aren't going to start with those. You're going to start with the easy ones, just as you did when you learned to write. When you were in the first grade nobody threw a pencil at you and said, "Write a compound sentence with at least sixteen words in it." They said, "This is a pencil, and this is how you hold it, and now let's spend an hour a day for the next couple of weeks drawing slanty lines until you begin to catch on." You started at the beginning and proceeded slowly, step by step, until it became practically automatic. The same with sleight of hand. You crawl first, and then you walk, and then, when you become good, you run like the wind!

Q. How do I get started in sleight of hand?

The best way is through books. There are a number of good books that explain basic sleights. I think one of the best is a book called *Now You See It, Now You Don't: Lessons in Sleight of Hand*, which, by odd coincidence, I happen to have written. I am mentioning it here not because I am trying to sell books, but because I sincerely think it is the best book on basic sleight of hand available so far. Why? Essentially because it has lots of good pictures—close to two thousand of them. They, and the simplified text, will lead you step by step through most of the basic sleights with cards, coins, balls, silks and so on, and teach you a number of good tricks accomplished by pure sleight of hand besides. But don't bother to get it unless you are prepared to do some serious practicing!

Q. Are there any really good self-working tricks?

There may be a few lurking somewhere, but virtually all of the really good effects require some help from you, and there never was a trick anywhere that didn't need good presentation to make it effective. If you are going to get into magic, you might as well reconcile yourself to the fact that there is effort involved, but then that's half the fun.

Q. Why shouldn't I tell how it's done?

For a lot of good reasons. To begin with, it is more fun not to. Besides, people don't really appreciate knowing how it's done. They may badger you for the secret, but when you break down and finally tell, they are usually disappointed. All you have really done is spoil their fun and yours.

Magic is now and always has been a very secretive pursuit. That is part of its intrigue. In the old days, magicians usually invented their own tricks, and they guarded those secrets carefully. Many magicians still do. It is true that nowadays secrets are more liberally dispensed than they used to be, but they are nonetheless still secrets. Magicians don't really mind letting fellow practitioners in on some of their methods, but they don't ever want them broadcast to laymen. After you have spent a lot of time and energy learning and practicing, neither will you.

Now perhaps you are thinking, how about this book? The answer to that is simple. You or someone you know had to go out and spend money to buy this book. You have to spend time and effort reading it. If your interest is stimulated and you become a magician, then you are welcome to our ranks. If you don't, chances are all you will really do is brouse through the book and learn how a few tricks are done. When you see a magician perform, the overwhelming odds are that he will fool you anyway, and besides, after having become aware of how much effort is involved, you will have learned to appreciate him all the more.

Q. Where can I find audiences to perform for?

There are more opportunities to do free magic shows than you can shake a wand at. Once the word gets out that you are a good magician, you'll be besieged with requests—clubs, social groups, school proms, scouting, birthday parties and so forth. Entertainment is a desirable commodity anywhere that people gather, so if you do a good act, you'll have plenty of opportunity to show it off.

Q. What is the best way to get a volunteer from the audience onstage?

Selecting a person from the audience to help you with an effect can sometimes be a ticklish business. If the person is too extroverted and hammy he can divert the audience's attention away from the trick; if he is a wise guy or a skeptic, he can make the trick difficult to perform; and if he is too quiet and withdrawn he can be a bore. Selecting the right person takes a good deal of experience. Ideally the helper should be friendly, bright and possibly just a trifle shy, but inducing that type to come onstage to help you often poses a problem. Kids are generally eager enough to assist, but adults are frequently hesitant, so finding a willing volunteer can sometimes slow up the proceedings.

As a consequence, magicians have developed techniques to circumvent the problem. Following are two methods that work quite well, although neither should be used on an obviously shy person who is apt to be embarrassed by your attention.

In the first, the magician addresses the audience as follows: "Would you hold up your hand, please? Just raise it so we can all see it. That's fine, but I think it would be better if we could all see you. Would you stand up for a moment, please? Just stand up. Would you step this way a bit? Right over here, please. As long as you are up this far, you might as well come up here with me."

Once you have gotten your potential helper to rise and to step over in your direction, it's a relatively simple matter to induce him or her to go the full route and join you onstage.

A second method that works well and is somewhat amusing besides is this: You pick up a hank of soft rope and toss one end to the person you would like to have join you, and then you literally pull him or her onstage.

"Would you take the end of that rope, please? Just hang on and don't let go until I tell you. Would you stand up a moment, please? Now hang on . . ."

Pull the person toward you, continuing to admonish him to hold on, and draw him onstage. Once he is onstage, treat him politely and respectfully, but remember that it's your show. You're the magician!

Q. Is it all right to change the tricks in this book?

Magic is a creative art. Magicians often invent the tricks they do or modify existing tricks to conform to their own requirements or desires. You should feel free to do the same with the tricks in this book. Think it through carefully and work out the details before you do, however. Ideally, a trick is like a small drama. It has a beginning and a middle and an end.

Q. Where can I meet other magicians?

If you live in a large city, there is a good chance it may have a magic shop, and that's the best way to make initial contacts. Spend some time there and you'll undoubtedly run into other magicians of various ages and degrees of expertise. Magicians are always looking for someone to take a card, so you shouldn't have too much trouble getting acquainted. If you do, introduce yourself to the proprietor, who is undoubtedly a magician himself, tell him you are into magic, and inquire about clubs. Magicians enjoy one another's company so much that they are always forming clubs and planning gatherings, and that's where the fun really is.

The magic shops in New York City I frequently drop by—the Flosso Hornmann Magic Company, which is the oldest magic store in the country, and Louis Tannen's, which is the largest—are like conventions on Saturday afternoons, and sometimes so crowded with magicians you practically have to stand on line to get in!

Q. Can I make money doing magic?

This question is premature to say the least, but the answer is, eventually, why not? After you have done lots and lots of free shows at various social functions, and have developed to the point where you are sure you are capable of doing really good professional magic, you'll find opportunities to do shows.

But don't even dream of it until you are ready, and don't do shows for money unless you are certain you can give your employers their money's worth. And don't undercut professional performers who depend on magic for their livelihood!

terms and miscellaneous information you should know

presentation

To magicians, presentation is simply the act of presenting a magic trick. The magician comes onstage, shows his props, explains what he is doing, and leads the audience from the beginning of the trick right through to the climax. That's presentation, and it is the most important aspect of a trick.

Presentation has little or nothing to do with the technical proficiency with which you perform a trick. Of course that's important, but presentation is primarily concerned with the manner in which you present the trick to your audience. Do you remember the expression "It's not what you do, it's the way that you do it"? That sums it all up. The most brilliantly conceived trick is totally meaningless if the audience doesn't understand what you are doing. It's like looking at a magnificent watercolor through a dirty glass. What good are all the subtle nuances of color if you can't see them? So what if the drawing is utter perfection, if you can't even tell that it's there?

Good presentation is clear, direct, easy to follow, and as interesting and absorbing as you can make it. Your goal when you present a magic trick is to entertain your audience. You can entertain them by making them laugh or by entrancing them with dazzling displays of skill or by intriguing them with puzzling or thought-provoking effects. The more entertaining you have been, the more effective a job you have done, and presentation is the key to it all.

A simple trick in the hands of a great showman is vastly more effective than a great trick in the hands of a poor one. The great illusionist Harry Blackstone did a trick in his act that is a good illustration of what I am trying to say. Blackstone did a great many huge illusions. He sawed girls in half and made them disappear and reappear and float through the air with the greatest of ease, and his audience loved it. He did one trick, however— not a huge illusion or a great death-defying mystery but an old, relatively simple effect called the Haunted Handkerchief—that tore down the house! It was just a spooky white handkerchief that peeked out of a box and hesitantly crawled down the side of the box to the floor, where it danced about to musical accompaniment, all to Blackstone's apparent consternation. It was his most outstanding trick!

Why? Not because it was the biggest trick or the most expensive trick or the most technically brilliant trick, but because Blackstone's presentation—his acting, his patter, the music: all the elements that went into presenting the trick to his audience—was so superbly done that the trick was a masterpiece and the highlight of his show.

misdirection

Misdirection is the act of diverting your audience's attention away from that which you do not want them to see to that which you do, and it can be accomplished in a number of ways. Suppose, for example, that you want to vanish the coin in your right hand. You pretend to pass it to your left hand, but you actually retain it in your right. Your left reacts exactly as though it has received the coin. It puffs out just as it would if it were holding it. Your right hand, in which the coin is palmed, is open and appears to be empty. You gaze intently at your left hand, in an attempt to make your audience do the same. Your attention, and your audience's, is focused on your left hand. That, in essence, is misdirection. When you slowly open your hand to reveal that the coin has vanished, your audience is surprised because everything you have done has led them to believe that there really was a coin there in the first place.

Another technique for misdirecting your audience involves the use of a cover-up move to disguise your real objective. For example, you reach down to your table to pick up your wand, but your real purpose is to palm a coin that you had hidden behind some object. A common—in fact, rather overworked—ploy is the use of "whoofle dust." Occasionally during your act you reach into your pocket for magic "whoofle dust," which is generally invisible but may take the form of salt or confetti, and you sprinkle it over the object that is to be the subject of some magical manifestation. When you want to get rid of a palmed coin or other such object, you merely reach into your pocket for some whoofle dust—an act which your audience has now grown accustomed to and is therefore no longer suspicious of—and in the process you get rid of the palmed article you no longer need.

Misdirection is the stratagem magicians most depend on to accomplish their tricks. The more adept you become at it, the better a magician you are going to be.

patter

Unless you are doing a manipulative act in pantomime, patter is very important. You can't do effective magic, whether onstage or in front of a few friends, if your presentation is punctuated with long, dull, sleep-provoking pauses. You have to attract your audience's attention and then hold that attention, and anything you do to allow it to drift away is detrimental to the effect you are trying to produce. Even if your trick is very exciting visually, patter is what keeps your audience interested.

Patter can go in different directions and be effective in each one. Some magicians do a lot of selling: "I want you to notice that there is nothing in my right hand. There is nothing in my left hand. I take the coin very slowly and very carefully and I place it into the little box right before your eyes so there can be no doubt about it . . ." and so on. In other words, they explain exactly what they are doing while they are doing it, and they make it as plain and as obvious as they can in order to keep the audience's attention riveted right on the trick.

Other magicians achieve the same results by using a storyteller approach: "Far away, in the mountain fastness of the Himalayas lived an ancient Buddhist monk whose sole possession in all the world was a small silver coin which had been a gift to him from the High Lama of Tibet. I watched, fascinated, as he took the silver coin and . . ."

Those with a feel for comedy might punctuate their patter for the same trick with a dozen jokes and be equally effective. The actual direction your patter takes isn't nearly as important as doing it well—and you will if you remember that your objective is to entertain your audience.

Perhaps the best clue to what good patter sounds like is found by watching and listening to good magicians perform. See magicians as often as you can. Watch them live and on television, observe carefully, and learn. Don't imitate. Just learn.

finger palming

Although I have tried to avoid the use of sleight of hand in this book, there are one or two effects in which it is necessary to conceal an object in your hand, and since they were too good not to include, you are going to have to learn how to do a finger palm.

Hold the object as illustrated, be relaxed and natural, and don't glance at your hand. If you don't, neither will any one else. Practice by keeping an object palmed while you go about your normal routine—walking, talking, eating, reading—and in a short while the finger-palmed object will feel so natural, you won't even know it's there.

about silks

The handkerchiefs magicians use are referred to as silks, although nylons would probably be more appropriate, since that is what most silks seem to be made of these days. They owe their widespread use to the fact that they easily compress into a very small space, they spring open when they are liberated from their confines, and they are bright, colorful and attractive.

Unfortunately they are also expensive. Silk scarves of various sizes and types make pretty fair substitutes, or if you are into hemming or know someone who is, you will probably save money by buying fine nylon by the yard.

about servantes

A servante is a tray-like device attached to the back of a table or chair. Magicians use them to secretly obtain or dispose of various objects during their acts. They are no longer as popular as they were, essentially because magicians who work in nightclubs and other areas where they are largely surrounded by their audience can no longer get away with their use.

If you are working on a stage or anywhere your audience is in front of you, and you carry your own table, consider the use of a servante. There are a great many tricks that require you to secrete objects on your table. In many instances, they would be better and more efficiently hidden on your servante.

notes on construction

All of the tricks in this book are available commercially in various dimensions, qualities and price ranges. Most of them, however, can be made at home without too much effort. I have tried to show you how, but bear in mind that the methods I have outlined are to a large extent only suggestions. Obviously there are many ways to achieve the same end results. For example, you might roll a Production Tube (page 48) out of paper or light, strong cardboard, or utilize a mailing tube or a round cracker tin with the end cut off or plastic if you prefer.

Your options are limitless. I have given you the essentials. Precisely how you proceed is a matter of personal preference. Just remember that your apparatus has to function properly. Dependability is absolutely essential, and since you and your props are on public display, neatness counts.

where to get parts

music wire	Comes in various thicknesses, is used for model-airplane landing gear and other parts, and is available at hobby shops.
beeswax	The basis for magician's wax. Used commercially to wax the thread used in shoemaking. Available at craft shops that sell leatherworker's supplies.
rubber cement	Best for gluing paper. Used by commercial artists. Available at any good stationery store or art supply house.
glue	Epoxy glues will hold almost anything. Most convenient is 5-Minute epoxy, which really does cure (set up) in about five minutes.
plastic tubes	The canister-type vacuum cleaners craftsmen use to keep their shops clean employ a strong, opaque, thin-walled plastic tube to extend the range of their hose. One I have is three inches in diameter and around three feet long, and is easily sawed into lengths. Ask your hardware dealer.

Plexiglass is available in large-diameter tubes, but they are generally clear, the walls are fairly heavy, and they are expensive and hard to obtain.

metal tubes   Really good small-diameter tubes (drainpipes, 1¼ to 2 inches) made of thin-walled brass, chromed or natural finish, are available at any plumber's supply house or well-stocked hardware store. For larger-diameter tubes, use round cracker tins or cans of various sizes. The fancy groceries department of your supermarket is your best source.

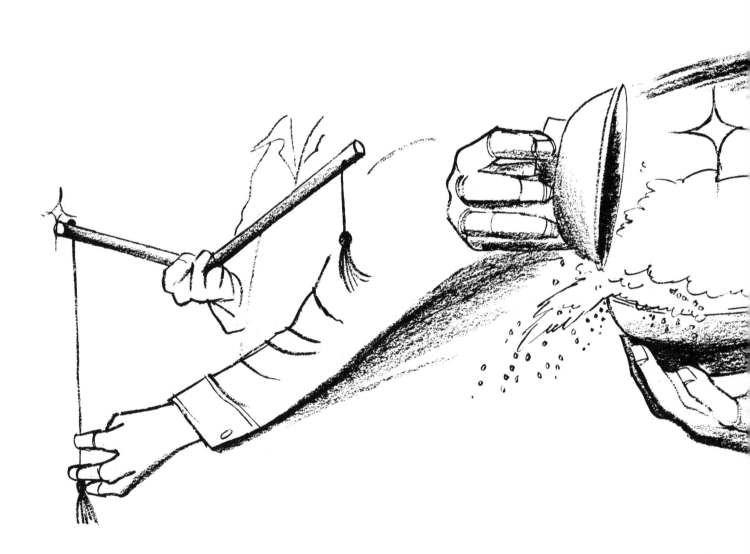

classic
magic tricks

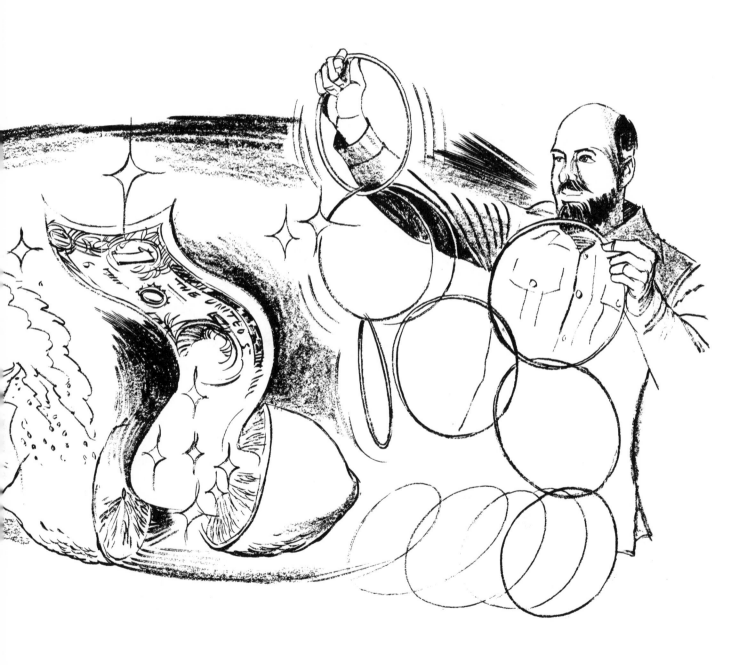

chinese rice bowls ★★★

*one of the great classics,
and still as miraculous as ever*

the effect

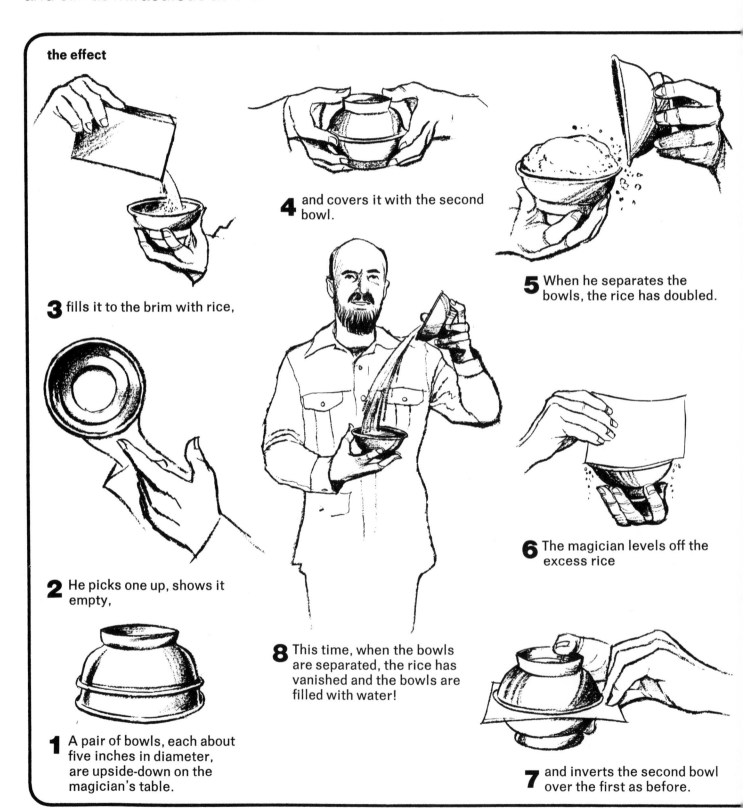

4 and covers it with the second bowl.

5 When he separates the bowls, the rice has doubled.

3 fills it to the brim with rice,

6 The magician levels off the excess rice

2 He picks one up, shows it empty,

8 This time, when the bowls are separated, the rice has vanished and the bowls are filled with water!

1 A pair of bowls, each about five inches in diameter, are upside-down on the magician's table.

7 and inverts the second bowl over the first as before.

to prepare

Chinese Rice Bowls are standard magic-shop items, but you can make your own easily enough. Obtain a matched pair of plastic or ceramic bowls about five or six inches in diameter (proportionately smaller if you have small hands). Japanese rice bowls are ideal.

Rub the mouth of the bowls over a sheet of 120-grit emery cloth until the rims have been sanded flat.

Lay one of the bowls over a sheet of clear, fairly flexible plastic about 3/64ths of an inch thick, and carefully trace the outline of the bowl with a sharp awl or heavy needle. Cut out the disc with a pair of heavy scissors, allowing a small tab to protrude.

Cut a cardboard or thin, opaque plastic square exactly as wide as the diameter of the disc plus the tab.

Rub a thin coating of Vaseline over the rim of one bowl (bowl A) and fill it almost to the rim with water. Place the plastic disc over the mouth and press it down firmly to force out as much air as possible. You should be able to pick up bowl A and turn it upside-down without spilling a drop.

Scatter a few matchsticks on your tabletop and place bowl A disc-down and tab towards the back, on top of them. (The matches or anything similar keep the disc from sticking to your tabletop.)

Place bowl B mouth-down over bowl A.

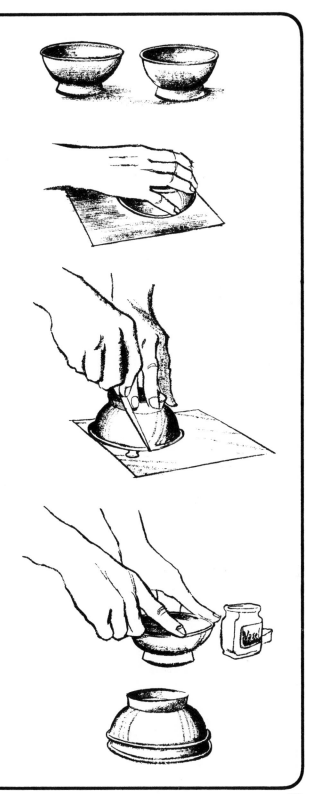

to perform

Pick up bowl B, show it to your audience, and fill it nearly to the brim with uncooked rice.

Place bowl A disc-down on top of bowl B, tab towards you, being careful not to show its interior.

Hold the bowls together, thumbs on top, fingers underneath, as you commune with the magic spirits by slowly moving the bowls through the air, finally turning them over so that bowl B is on top.

Remove bowl B. A is seen to be overflowing with rice. (Unless it doesn't matter if the floor gets messed up, work over your table, or better still, over a tray on your table.)

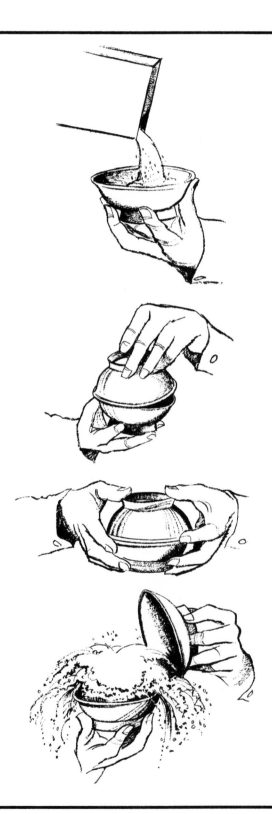

Set bowl B on your table, and with bowl A in your left hand, pick up the card with your right and use it to smooth the rice level with the rim.

Leave the card on bowl A and place bowl B mouth-down on top of it.

Holding both bowls in the left hand, fingers underneath and thumb on top, place right thumb on the underside of the disc tab and your right fingertips on top of card, carefully slide both out together, and place on your table, disc side down. (This move is tricky and takes practice to perform smoothly.)

If your hands aren't large enough to manage, you can remove the card and disc while the bowls are on your table.

Again describe a circle in the air with the bowls (but gently, or the water may spurt out). Without turning the bowls over, lift B off A and pour the water from bowl to bowl!

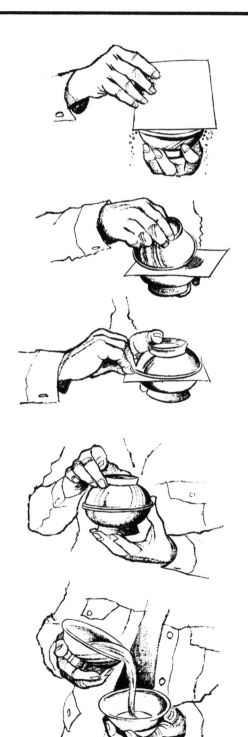

the dollar bill in the lemon ★★★

a dynamite trick that really leaves audiences totally perplexed

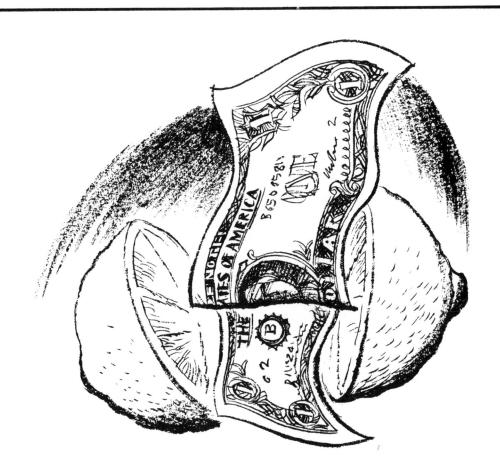

the effect

The magician displays a lemon and tosses it to someone in the audience to hold. He borrows a dollar bill, has the serial number recorded, places the bill in a small envelope and unmistakably burns it. He cuts open the lemon in full view of the audience, and finds the missing bill within. The serial number checks out and the bill is returned to the lender.

1 Jot down the serial number of a fairly new dollar bill and fold in half lengthwise, and in half again widthwise.

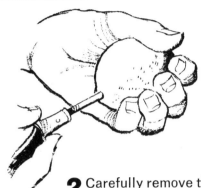

2 Carefully remove the pip from a lemon, and poke a hole in the lemon with an ice pick or a large nail.

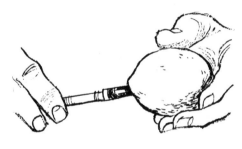

3 Roll the bill into a tight little package and push it into the middle of the lemon with the blunt end of a pencil.

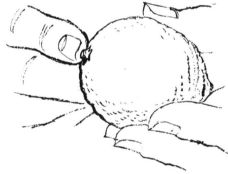

4 Carefully glue the pip back into place with Elmer's glue, airplane glue or any other glue you have that works.

5 Cut a neat slit in the back of a small coin envelope as illustrated.

6 Tear the edge off a dollar bill and paste it under the flap of the envelope.

7 Have an ashtray and a sharp knife on your table, and a good lighter or a few wooden matches in your left jacket pocket.

to perform

Toss the lemon to any member of your audience and ask him to hold it until you need it.

Borrow a dollar bill.

Hand a pad and pencil, or better yet, a Magic Marker and a piece of white illustration board to a member of the audience, and ask him to write down the serial number of the dollar bill you have just borrowed as you read it off to him.

Actually you call off the serial number of the bill which you have previously inserted into the lemon. If you have difficulty in memorizing the number, write it on your thumbnail and rub it off when you are finished.

Fold the dollar bill in half and half again. Insert it into the envelope, out through the slit in the back, and into your left hand. Take the envelope in your right hand and turn it around so the audience can see the edge of the pasted-in bill.

At the same time, reach into your left jacket pocket for your matches or lighter with your left hand, leaving the palmed bill behind.

Strike a match and light the envelope. When the flames get too close to your fingers, let it finish burning in your ashtray.

Ask for the lemon, show your hands unmistakably empty, and in full view of your audience, cut the lemon apart and have the lender remove his dollar from the lemon.

Ask him to slowly read the serial number of the bill and have the person who wrote the number down confirm it.

F18278954E

chinese wands ★

*an old favorite and one of the
best "children's magic" tricks ever*

the effect

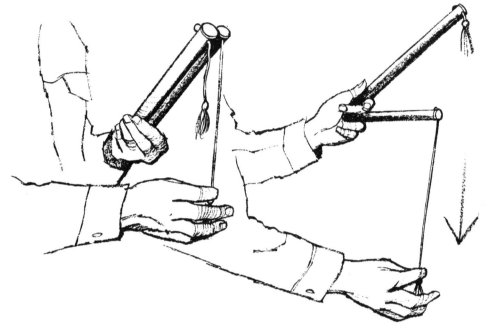

1 The magician holds two wands with a
tasseled cord running through each end.

2 When one cord is pulled down, the other rises,
and vice versa.

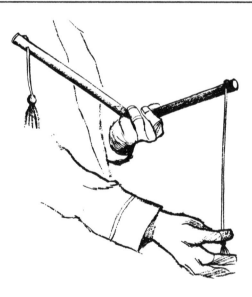

3 At the audience's request, the magician
separates the sticks, but the same thing
occurs.

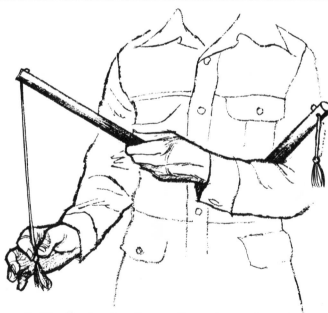

4 Finally, to stop the audience's continued
protests, the magician holds the sticks far
apart, but the long cord still rises mysteriously
when the short one is pulled down!

to prepare

Chinese Wands are available in a wide variety of sizes and prices, but you can make your own without too much trouble.

Obtain two hollow rods of thin-walled plastic, aluminum or brass. Size is a matter of personal preference.

Drill a $\frac{3}{32}$-inch hole about $\frac{1}{2}$ inch from one end of each rod and smooth the edges.

Obtain a length of cold rolled steel or brass rod and cut two pieces, each about one-quarter as long as your sticks.*

Drill the end of the rods, and epoxy or solder in a screw-eye.

Slip a strong, thin tasseled cord through the holes and the screw of each wand.

Cap the ends and paint or otherwise decorate both sticks.

* Use only as much weight as you need to bring up the tassel smoothly. Cut off the excess.

Hold rods side by side. One cord is extended full length and the other is as short as possible.

Explain that when one cord is pulled down the other rises up, and demonstrate several times. (As you pull the short cord down, unobtrusively raise the ends of the wands and the sliding weights will pull the cord up for you.)

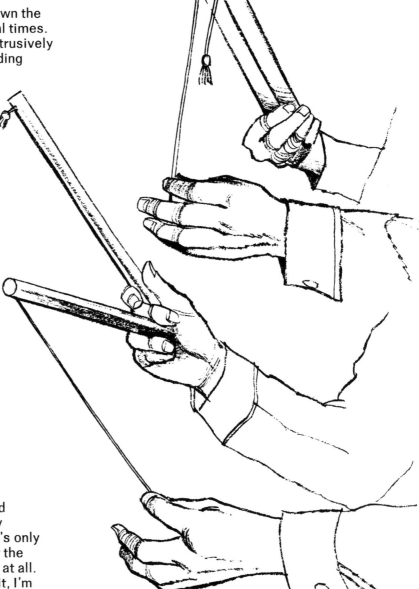

Your audience will appear skeptical and unimpressed. Say, "You don't look very impressed. Oh, I know. You think there's only one cord going right through the end of the wands. Right? Well, that's not the case at all. This is a real magic trick, and to prove it, I'm going to separate the wands."

Separate the wands. "There! How's that? I pull down the short cord and it becomes long. See? As this one comes down, this one comes up!"

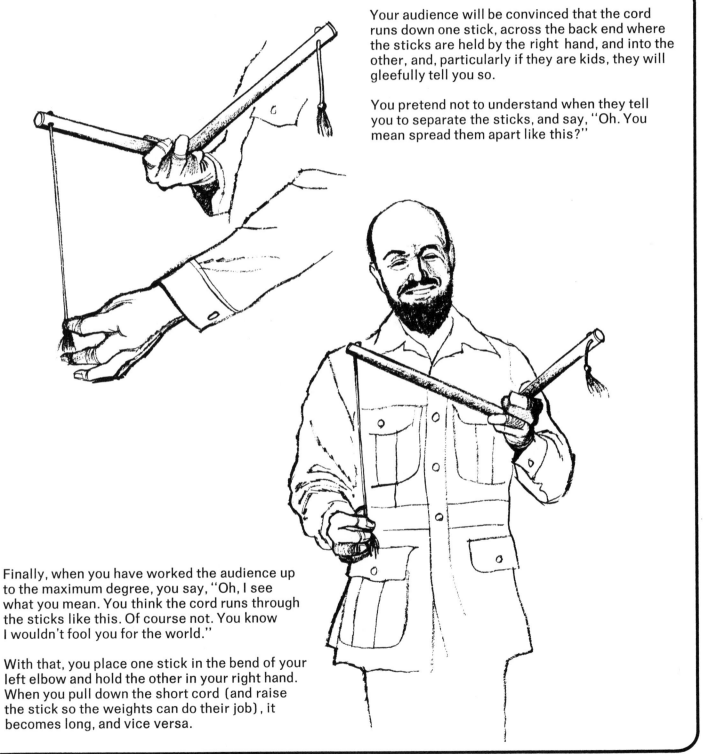

Your audience will be convinced that the cord runs down one stick, across the back end where the sticks are held by the right hand, and into the other, and, particularly if they are kids, they will gleefully tell you so.

You pretend not to understand when they tell you to separate the sticks, and say, "Oh. You mean spread them apart like this?"

Finally, when you have worked the audience up to the maximum degree, you say, "Oh, I see what you mean. You think the cord runs through the sticks like this. Of course not. You know I wouldn't fool you for the world."

With that, you place one stick in the bend of your left elbow and hold the other in your right hand. When you pull down the short cord (and raise the stick so the weights can do their job), it becomes long, and vice versa.

the chinese rings ★

the effect

Eight solid steel rings—examined by the audience—mysteriously link and unlink at the magicians command.

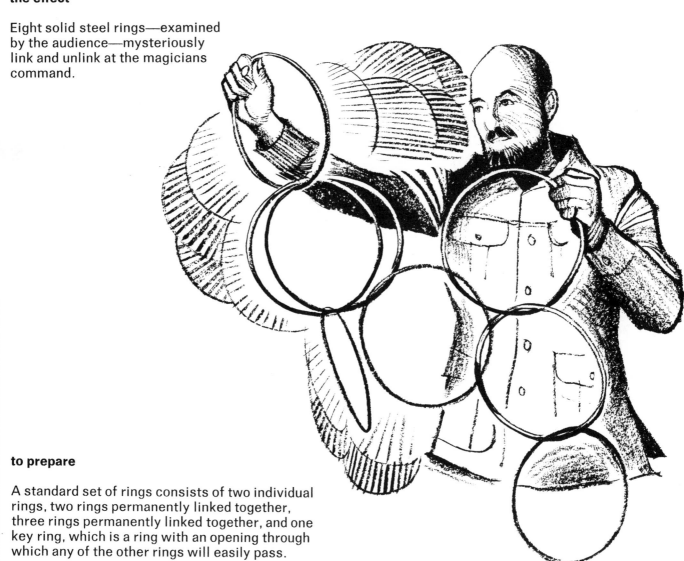

to prepare

A standard set of rings consists of two individual rings, two rings permanently linked together, three rings permanently linked together, and one key ring, which is a ring with an opening through which any of the other rings will easily pass.

to perform

Hold the rings in your right hand in this order, starting at your fingertips: two separate rings, group of two, group of three, and last (next to your wrist), the key ring.

Assume position with your left side towards the audience, hold the rings at shoulder height in your right hand, and count—you have to create the illusion that each ring is separate.

1 Hold your left hand below the rings and drop the first single ring into your left hand. Catch it in your left and lower your left as you catch it, counting "one."

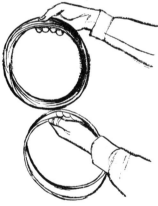

2 Repeat with the second single ring, counting "two."

3 Bring the left hand up, hold it still, and release one of the set of two, counting "three."

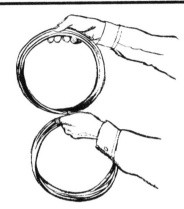

4 Drop the second ring of the set of two, lowering your hand as you catch it, counting "four."

5 Bring the left up, hold it still, and release one of the set of three, counting "five."

6 Repeat with the second of the set of three, counting "six."

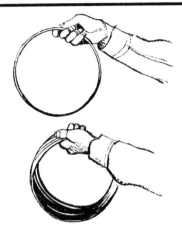

7 Drop the third, lowering your left hand as you catch it, counting "seven."

8 As your left hand comes up, slap the key ring onto the stack of rings, counting "eight."

9 Transfer the rings back to your right hand, key ring on the inside next to your wrist.

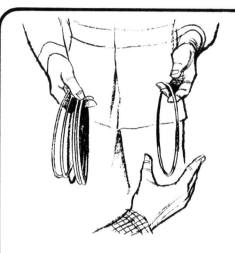

10 Invite two spectators up and with one on either side of you, hand each a single ring, and invite them to examine them thoroughly.

11 Meanwhile, transfer the rings to your left hand, key ring on the inside next to your wrist. Thumb and first finger hold all the rings but one of the group of two, which lies on the second, third and fourth fingers.

12 Take the single ring from the spectator on your left and hand it to the person on your right, requesting that he link the two together.

13 Obviously he can't. Hand the rings to the spectator on your left with the request that he link them together.

14 Take back one single ring, and with your left side to the audience, show how the rings are linked by striking the single ring into your left hand where it joins the others between the third and first fingers.

15 At the instant of contact, allow one ring from the set of two in your left hand to fall. You have apparently linked the single ring.

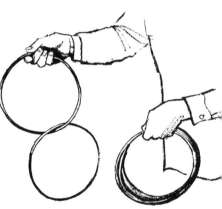

16 Immediately grasp the dangling ring, and pulling it and its mate away, hand it to the spectator on your right, saying, "That's what I asked you to do."

17 Take the single ring from the spectator on your right.

18 As you do so, slip the first finger of the left hand between the two inner and the outer ring of the group of three so that the latter lies on the second, third and fourth fingers. The key, group of three, and single are held between the left thumb and first finger.

19 Strike the single ring against the group as before, grasping it between the left thumb and first fingers and immediately allow the outermost of the group of three to fall.

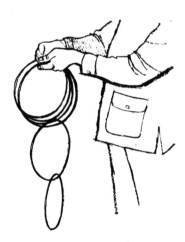

20 Take the outermost of the single rings in the right hand and strike it into the bunch as in 19, retaining it between the left first and second fingers, and immediately allow the second ring in the group of three to fall.

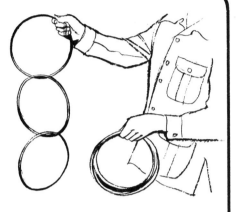

21 Hand the group of three to the spectator on your left.

22 Transfer the two individual rings and the key ring singly from the left to right hand.

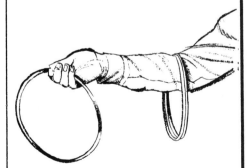

23 Allow the two single rings to slide down your right arm.

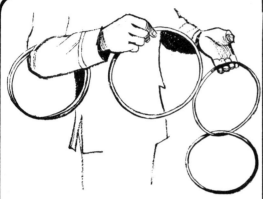

24 Hold the key ring in your right hand. Take the set of two with your left.

25 Transfer the key ring to the left hand so that the opening is held over the outer ring between the thumb and the left first finger.

26 Pass one single to each assistant.

27 As you do so, slip the key over the rings in your left and let the rings drop, one by one, to reveal a set of three. Keep the key in your left hand and hide the opening between the left thumb and first and second fingers.

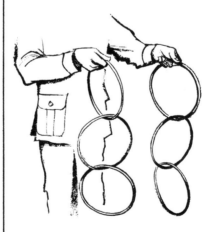

28 Take back the set of three in the right hand from the spectator on your left.

29 With one chain dangling from your left and one from your right, slowly bring the hands together and link the chains.

30 Hold the key in the right hand, opening behind the right fingers, grasp the bottom of the chain of three in your left, and raise left arm full length overhead. The right fingers remain positioned loosely over the opening in the key ring.

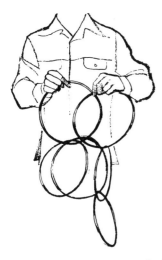

31 Release the top ring held in the left hand, allowing the chain of three and two to dangle from the key ring, which is held by the right.

32 Pick up the top ring of the chain of three with the left hand, and unlink.

33 Slip the left arm through the top ring of the chain of three.

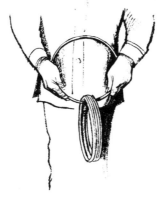

34 Pick up the top ring of the chain of two and unlink.

35 Hand the chain of two to the helper on your left.

36 Link the top ring of the chain of three to the key ring.

37 Take back the chain of two and link one ring to the key ring.

38 Rapidly link the other rings to the key ring until all the rings are joined together.

39 You may conclude your routine at this point, or, as is frequently done, you may shake all the rings loose from the key ring and let them clatter to the floor.

That is a basic Chinese Ring routine. Some magicians use a great many embellishments, including the following. Others do simple versions utilizing no more than four or five rings. After you become involved with the trick, you'll probably want to create your own routine.

rope and bottle trick ★★

*an old-time favorite — simple,
ingenious and very perplexing*

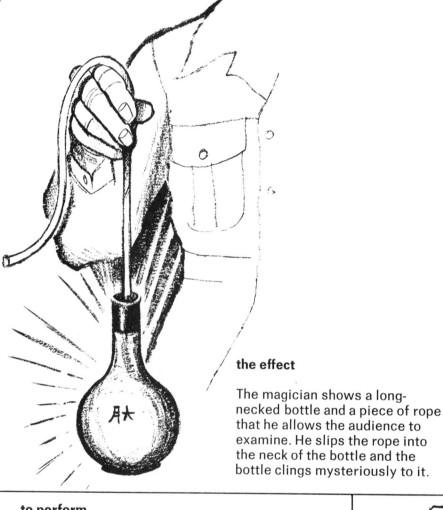

to prepare

Obtain a couple of feet of fairly
soft clothesline, a solid rubber
ball about a half-inch in diameter,
and a bottle about eight inches
tall, and ideally, shaped as
illustrated. (Olive oil frequently
comes in bottles of precisely
this shape.)

Enamel the bottle (red is the
traditional color) and paint on a
Chinese character or two.

the effect

The magician shows a long-
necked bottle and a piece of rope
that he allows the audience to
examine. He slips the rope into
the neck of the bottle and the
bottle clings mysteriously to it.

to perform

1 The bottle, rope and ball are on your table, the
ball hidden from view behind the rope.

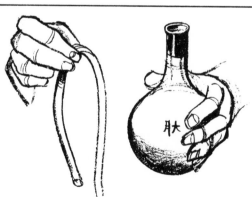

2 Pick up the bottle with your left hand and
finger-palm the ball as you pick up the rope
with your right.

3 Pass the bottle to a member of your audience for examination.

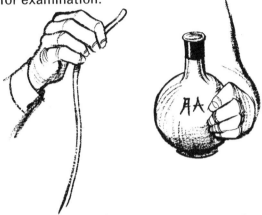

4 Take the bottle back with your left hand and pass the rope to a spectator with your right, retaining the ball in a finger palm.

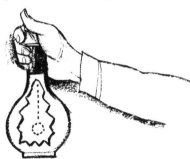

5 Immediately pass the bottle to your right hand and secretly drop the ball into it.

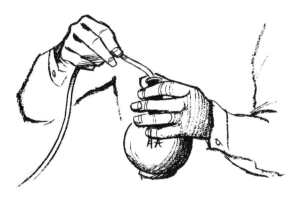

6 Transfer the bottle to your left, take the rope with your right, and insert about six inches of the rope into the neck.

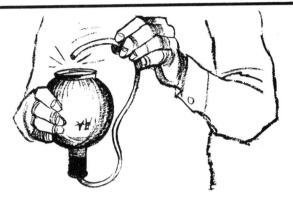

7 Turn the bottle upside-down, and tap the bottom of the bottle with the rope as you say the magic word.

8 Release the bottle and it swings on the rope!

(To release the rope, push it into the neck of the bottle when the bottle is right side up.)

You have just performed a basic Rope and Bottle routine. After you have practiced for a bit and can get the ball in and out of the bottle confidently and well, you can elaborate on the routine by allowing members of the audience to try (and fail) to get the rope to cling.

Just remember to carefully work out all of your moves in advance and practice them well. And remember, *misdirection* is what it's all about!

the drumhead tube ★★★

a classic silk production

the effect

The magician caps the end of an empty tube with sheets of tissue paper. He waves his wand, breaks through the tissue and produces a number of silks.

to prepare

Obtain a ten-ounce plastic drinking tumbler and roll a stiff sheet of paper into a tube the identical diameter of the mouth of the tumbler (generally three inches), and about twelve inches long. (A cardboard mailing tube or thin plastic or metal tube would be better.)

Make two rings out of cardboard, plastic or metal that will fit snugly over your tube, or use rubber bands.

Fold a number of silks and load into the tumbler.

Use a rubber band to affix a sheet of tissue over the tumbler mouth.

Place the tumbler mouth-down on your table, hidden behind one of your props.

Place the rings or rubber bands and two eight-by-eight-inch sheets of matching tissue on your table along with the empty tube.

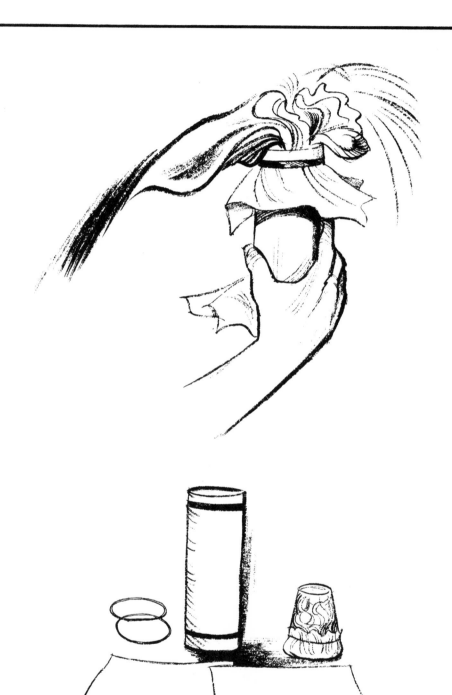

to perform

1 Pick up the tube in your left hand and show that it is unmistakably empty.

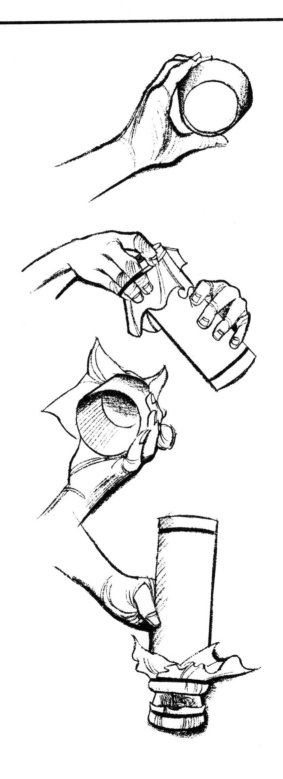

2 Pick up a sheet of tissue with your right, show it on all sides, and affix it to one end of the tube with a ring or rubber band.

3 Turn the tube around and let your audience see into it again.

4 Casually set the tube down directly on top of the inverted tumbler with enough force to break through the tissue and lodge the tumbler securely in place.

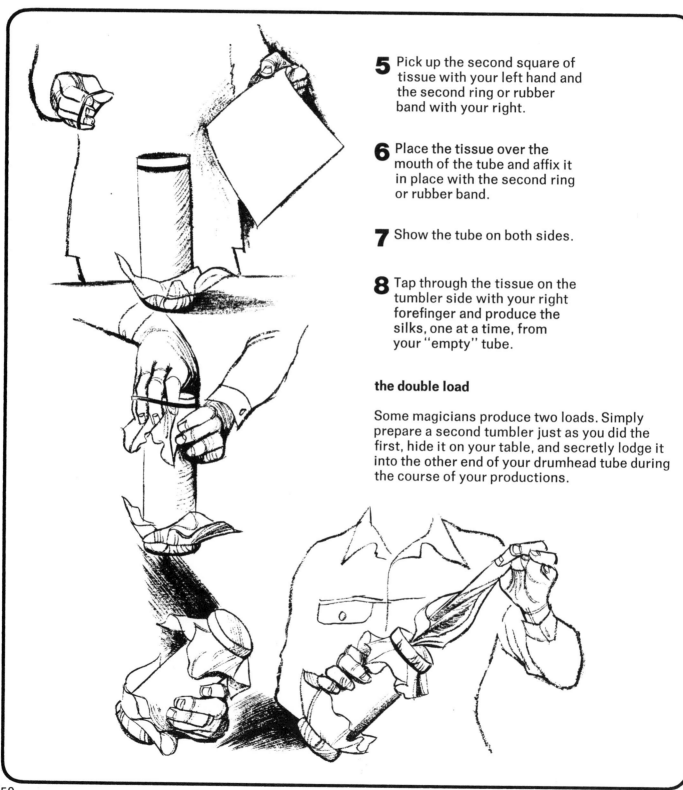

5 Pick up the second square of tissue with your left hand and the second ring or rubber band with your right.

6 Place the tissue over the mouth of the tube and affix it in place with the second ring or rubber band.

7 Show the tube on both sides.

8 Tap through the tissue on the tumbler side with your right forefinger and produce the silks, one at a time, from your "empty" tube.

the double load

Some magicians produce two loads. Simply prepare a second tumbler just as you did the first, hide it on your table, and secretly lodge it into the other end of your drumhead tube during the course of your productions.

the inexhaustible hat ★★★

Hat productions were once extremely popular. Rare was the old-time magician who didn't produce at least one cannonball from his empty hat during the course of his show. *Programs of Famous Magicians*, a fascinating little turn-of-the-century volume by J. F. Burroughs, lists the program of Hartz, who produced the following items from his "inexhaustible hat":

ARTICLES PRODUCED — Two dozen silk handkerchiefs, a baby's bodice, twenty-five silvered goblets, eighteen pint tumblers, a wig, eight cigar boxes, a bowl of gold fish, a china flower vase, twelve champagne bottles, a large bird cage, seven pounds weight of playing cards, one hundred yards of silk sash ribbon, six glass lanterns, a Japanese doll, crinoline and a skull.

Various hat-fakes have been designed to make a "loaded" hat look empty, but they are rarely used. In the overwhelming majority of cases, the hat really is empty and the rabbit or whatever is secretly loaded into it.

You can show an empty hat, produce your rabbit, and take your bows at that point, or you can go on to produce a wide variety of other items, as Hartz and so many others did. Essentially you show your hat empty, steal a load, and produce an array of silks, balls, flowers and so on. As the various items come tumbling from your hat in apparently endless array, you steal other loads, one from your body, one from the back of your chair, perhaps another from your table, and soon you have covered the stage with the contents of your inexhaustible hat.

Following are a few of the many ways to accomplish this. In every one of them, the real secret is misdirection. Steals always have to be made while the audience's attention is diverted away from the action taking place—not too difficult a problem if you work your moves out carefully.

the cape load

Although your chances of working in a full dress suit and a cape are probably remote, here is an excellent rabbit production opener.

The rabbit bag (and rabbit) is slung on a hook sewn to your cape, which is thrown over your arm. You enter stage left, pause at midstage, remove your top hat and show it unmistakably empty. In the act of setting your cape down on your chair, you scoop the rabbit into your hat, reach in and produce it. The bag remains in the hat, unseen.

The same general method would work just as well if you were wearing a soft hat and carrying a top coat or a raincoat, and of course you don't have to produce a rabbit. Silks or other production items will work well too.

back of the chair load

In this case your load—a rabbit in a bag, or whatever—is hanging from a headless nail on the back of a chair onstage. As you bend over to pick up your wand on the seat of the chair, or as you deposit some object on the seat—preferably something you have just produced from your hat—you steal the load and swing it right into your hat in one smooth, deft and well-practiced motion.

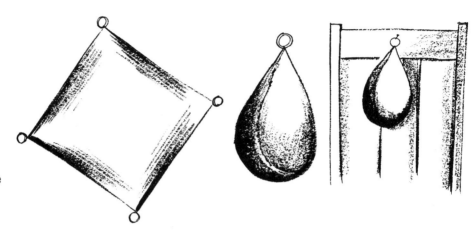

from your assistant

If you are working with an assistant, you can steal a load from her back. As you hand her items you have just produced, your hat momentarily passes behind her back or behind the tray she is holding, and the deed is done!

body loads

There are various techniques by which a body load consisting of anything from a rabbit to a glass of water can be loaded into your hat. Ideally you should work out your own specific method, plan it well, and practice it to utter perfection.

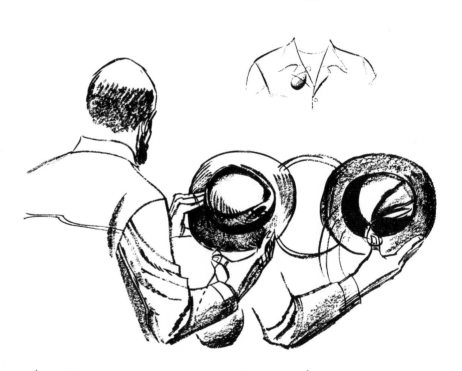

You show your hat empty, reach into the air with your right hand as though catching some invisible object, and as you do so your left hand crosses your body, your thumb engages the protruding wire loop, and the load is popped into your hat.

table load

You show your hat empty, set it down on your table, and in the process catch the protruding loop from your load, which automatically swings into your hat as you set it down.

traditional production items

silks—colorful, attractive and highly compressible.

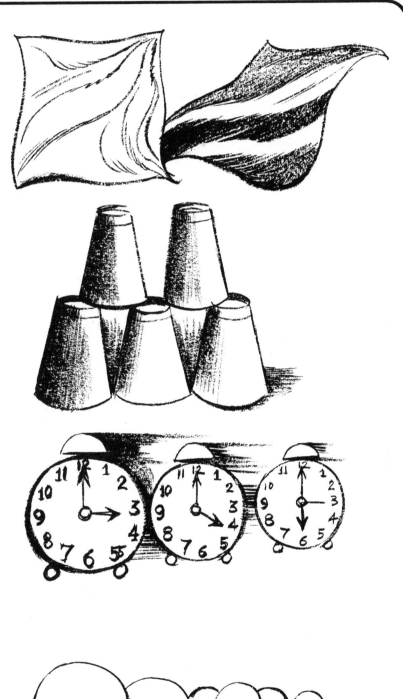

tin goblets—they nest closely, are flashy, and really bulk out after they are produced, but alas, they are no longer made. Thin, opaque plastic glasses are substitutes.

alarm clocks—they are faked to nest inside each other. Silks or spring-flowers utilize leftover space.

pop balls—they are made of paper, are four inches in diameter and pop open automatically, and a large number of them fold into a small package.

canned goods—they nest together and you can easily make
your own. Cut off tops, remove
contents, leave on labels and
clean well before using.

sausages—strings of cloth,
spring-activated sausages are
highly compressible and look
funny (but rarely authentic)
coming from a hat.

In recent years modern technology has contributed such hat
production items as melons, cabbages, and other assorted fruits,
vegetables, bottles, and so forth. These are made of thin latex,
generally molded from the genuine item, and are skillfully
painted and hence quite real-looking.

funny animals—"scrawny" chickens, skunks,
rabbits and other unlikely-looking specimens are
also produced from hats for comedy effect.

spring-flowers—a large bouquet
twelve to fifteen inches in
diameter can compress into a
package no more than three
inches or so across and an inch
and a half deep.

balloons—self-inflating balloons are reputed to make good production items, but I've never tried them.

In *Greater Magic*, Caryl Fleming reveals a good method suggested to him by the Great Leon.

good-quality rubber balloons, size 7

Bangsite, the acetylene-producing powder used in toy cannons

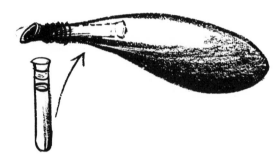

one-dram glass vial filled with water and corked

one dram of loose Bangsite in each balloon

tie ends of balloons with coarse cotton thread.

After the balloons are introduced into your hat, pop the cork out to release the water. Water mixes with Bangsite and the resulting gas blows up the balloons, which you then produce.

Experiment, but be careful. Acetylene is highly flammable, and it smells bad.

hat coils—a large coiled paper streamer that makes a huge pile of colorful paper ribbon.

spring-rabbit—a real-fur spring-constructed compressible rabbit that looks and acts quite authentic.

the cut and restored turban ★★★

a great trick, but it takes time and effort to master

the effect

The magician exhibits a long turban that is held at each end by an assistant from the audience. One of the assistants cuts the turban into two pieces, the cut ends are tied together, and at the magic word the knot vanishes and the turban is restored!

to prepare

Obtain a length of cheesecloth or any thin, inexpensive cloth approximately fifteen feet long and about a foot and a half wide. Use it white, or if you prefer, dye it with Tintex.

to perform

1 Ask two volunteers from the audience to join you onstage.

2 Show the cloth, explain that it is actually a Hindu turban, hand an end to each assistant and have them stretch it out between them.

3 Position yourself behind and at the center of the turban.

4 Grasp the center of the turban in your left hand.

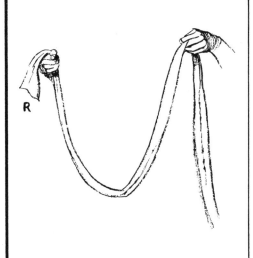

5 Take end R in your right hand from the assistant on your right and bring it in front of the center portion.

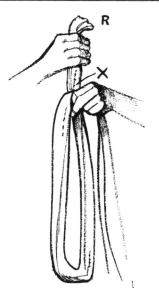

6 Grasp the turban at X with your left hand and

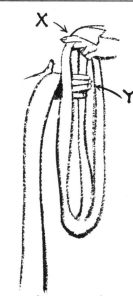

7 Grasp the vertical piece with your right hand at point Y and

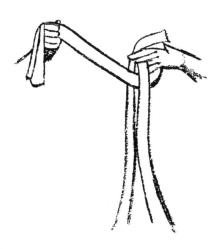

8 carry it over to your right.

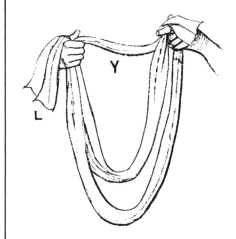

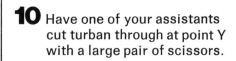

9 Have assistant on your left hand you end L, which you hold in your right hand.

10 Have one of your assistants cut turban through at point Y with a large pair of scissors.

11 While each assistant loosely holds an end, tie a simple knot into the center of the turban that holds the short piece in place.

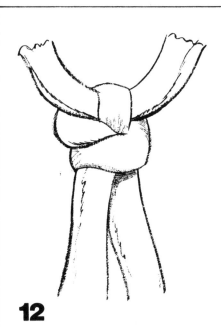

12

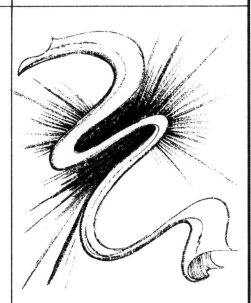

13 Trim away the short piece.

14 Open the knot and have your assistants pull the restored turban taut.

dyeing the silks ★★★

one of the great silk tricks
of all time

the effect

The magician shows a sheet of white paper on both sides. He rolls the paper into a tube, secures it with a rubber band, and pokes a white silk through it. The silk comes out white just the way it went in. When the magician pokes it through a second time it emerges red, another white silk comes out blue, and a third is mysteriously dyed green. The magician unrolls the tube and it is seen to be unmistakably empty.

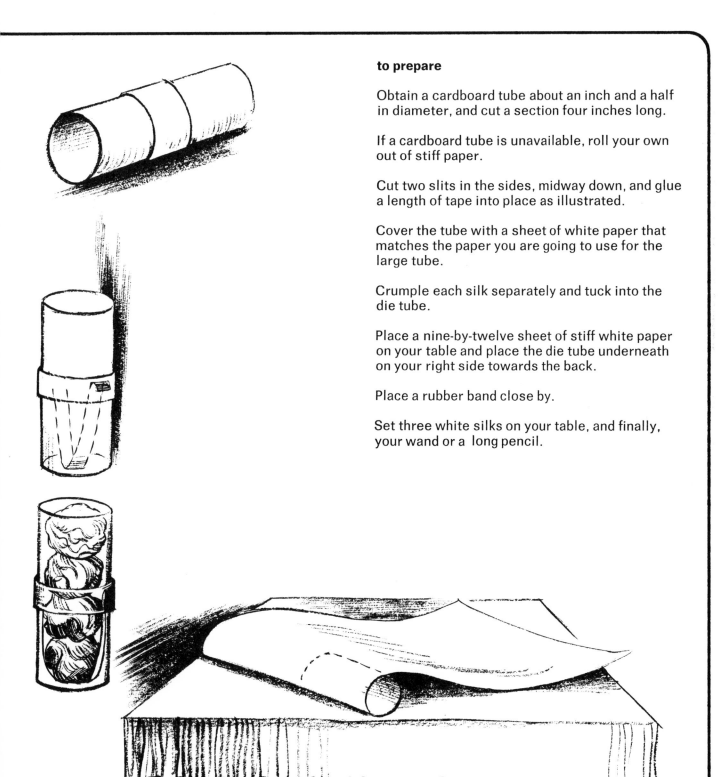

to prepare

Obtain a cardboard tube about an inch and a half in diameter, and cut a section four inches long.

If a cardboard tube is unavailable, roll your own out of stiff paper.

Cut two slits in the sides, midway down, and glue a length of tape into place as illustrated.

Cover the tube with a sheet of white paper that matches the paper you are going to use for the large tube.

Crumple each silk separately and tuck into the die tube.

Place a nine-by-twelve sheet of stiff white paper on your table and place the die tube underneath on your right side towards the back.

Place a rubber band close by.

Set three white silks on your table, and finally, your wand or a long pencil.

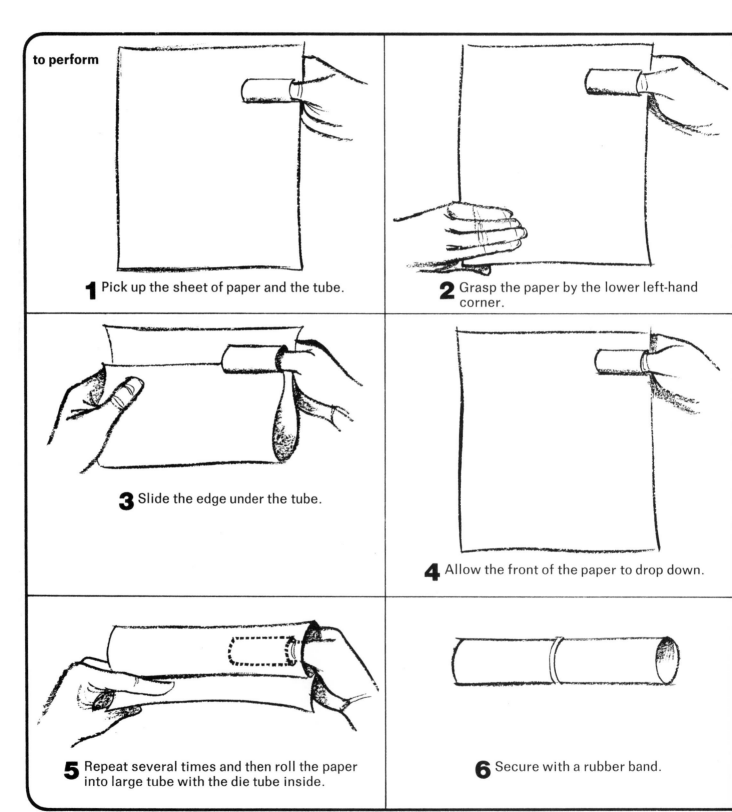

1 Pick up the sheet of paper and the tube.

2 Grasp the paper by the lower left-hand corner.

3 Slide the edge under the tube.

4 Allow the front of the paper to drop down.

5 Repeat several times and then roll the paper into large tube with the die tube inside.

6 Secure with a rubber band.

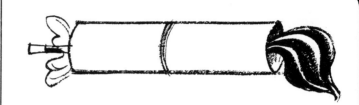

7 Poke a white silk through the tube. It emerges white, proving that your tube is empty.

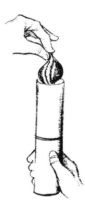

8 Poke the white silk back through the tube. This time it emerges red.

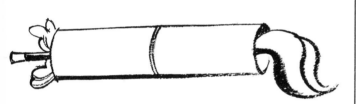

9 Repeat with the next two silks.

10 As the last silk is pulled through, hold it up with your left hand, and simultaneously bring the die tube to a vertical position over your table with your right hand,

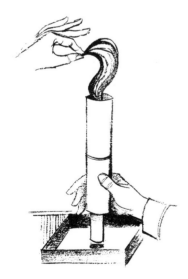

11 allowing the die tube to slip out and fall onto your servante or behind some object on your table.

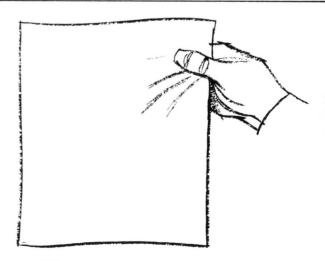

12 Open the tube and show it empty.

card on the ribbon penetration★★

a mystery that will have your audience gasping in astonishment

the effect

The magician has a member of the audience select a card from an ordinary deck. He shows an envelope, pokes a hole through its center, strings a ribbon through the hole, and then openly places the selected card into the envelope, which he then seals.

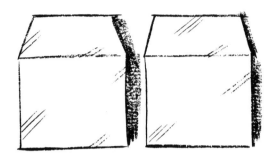

He grasps both ends of the ribbon, pulls smartly, and announces that the ribbon has penetrated the card. He tears off the envelope, and sure enough, the selected card is seen dangling on the ribbon.

to prepare

Obtain two heavy, unlined, Monarch-type envelopes (the squarish kind) no less than four inches high, and sufficiently opaque so that a card cannot be seen through it.

Neatly cut the face and attached flap of one envelope about one-sixteenth of an inch from each edge and set aside.

Take one of the cards from your deck (of which you have a duplicate), place a tiny dab of rubber cement on the back at one corner, and place the card in the envelope, back towards the flap-side.

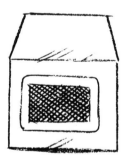

Insert the extra face into the envelope on top of the card, wet the gummed surface of the first envelope and glue the flaps together.

Place a sharp, narrow, pointed knife, a three-foot length of one-half-inch ribbon, and a deck of cards on your table.

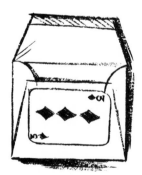

to perform

Invite a spectator on stage to help you.

Ask him to select a card. (Actually force the duplicate as instructed in No-Skill Card Force, page 106.)

Then say, "Will you please show us the card you selected? Just hold it up so we can all see it. It doesn't matter if I know the card."

Put the deck down, and pick up the envelope and the knife. Push the blade through the center of the envelope (and of course the duplicate card), and twist slightly to make a hole large enough for the ribbon to easily pass through.

Thread the ribbon through the hole and show the spectator and your audience the interior of the envelope.

Openly place the selected card into the envelope, turn the envelope with the back towards the audience, and secretly stand the card on end at one side of the envelope away from the ribbon.

Moisten the flap, seal the envelope, say the magic words, and grasping one end of the ribbon in each hand, snap your hands apart.

"I think that may have done it . . . It felt as though the ribbon actually penetrated the chosen card. Let's see."

Tear open the end of the envelope opposite the duplicate card, show the inside to your helper and the audience, and slowly reach in, pull out and display the selected card.

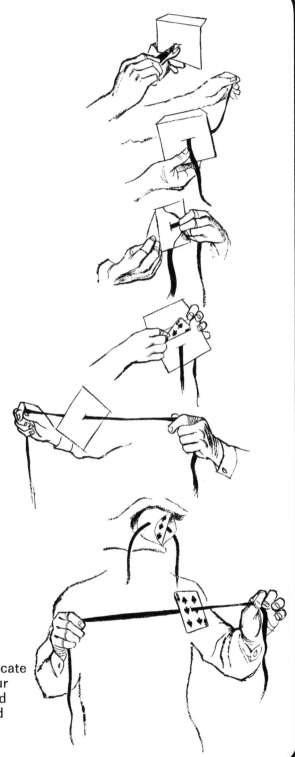

the vanishing bowl of water ★★★

a spectacular, and most ingenious, vanish

the effect

The magician pours a pitcher of water into a bowl resting on a tray held by his assistant. He covers the bowl with a cloth, removes it from the tray, and tosses it into the air. The cloth floats down empty. The bowl of water has vanished!

to prepare

The original bowls sold in magic shops were made of metal, but you can make one of plastic that will work just as well. Obtain a plastic bowl about eight inches in diameter (avoid polyethylene or any other waxy-surfaced plastic to which glue won't adhere).

Trace the outline of the bowl on a sheet of clear plastic with an awl or heavy needle, cut it to shape but slightly smaller in diameter, and trim off the end as illustrated.

Glue the trimmed disc in place, and note that it slants down slightly to enable excess water to run off. I have found that 5-Minute epoxy forms a strong waterproof bond, but just to be sure, caulk the glued seam with white silicone rubber.

Make or obtain two metal fittings—one to affix to the bottom of the bowl and the other to the tray.

If your bowl doesn't have a rim around the base, the metal fitting affixed to the bottom will keep it from sitting level. One solution is to glue on a rim.

Unless you are absolutely certain that your glue will hold (and actual testing is the only way to tell), then drill two 1/8-inch holes through your fitting and the bowls, and bolt it in place, using plenty of silicone rubber to prevent leakages.

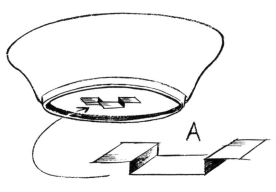

A

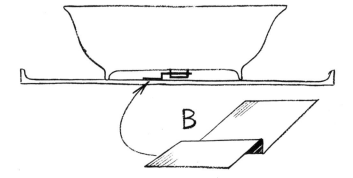

B

Your tray should be sufficiently wider than the bowl to hide it well. Glue the other fitting to the center of the tray, or better still, bolt it on too.

The cloth you use for the vanish must be opaque, even in the glare of a bright spotlight. A double thickness is best.

Cut a disc of thin, stiff plastic to the exact outline of your bowl and sew it in the center of the cloth. A thin wire hoop the size of the bowl will work as well.

to perform

Have your assistant come onstage carrying a tray with your vanishing bowl and a pitcher of water.

Pick up the bowl with your left hand, but don't show the inside, and pick up the pitcher with your right. Replace the bowl on the tray, smoothly slipping the fitting on the bowl into the one on the tray.

Fill the bowl with a thin stream of water poured from a height of a foot or so.

Set the pitcher down on your table, pick up the cloth, and toss it over the bowl so that the disc coincides with the mouth of the bowl.

Remove the cloth, and apparently the bowl, with both hands. (The disc makes it appear as though the bowl is under the cloth.)

As you lift the cloth away, your assistant pivots the tray in a very natural manner, drops it to her side, and unobtrusively walks offstage as you, apparently holding the bowl, step forward. This move has to be practiced to perfection.

Actually remove the bowl a number of times, carefully noting the effect in a mirror. When you leave the bowl behind, every move must look precisely as it did when you actually took it.

Toss the cloth in the air and catch it on the way down. The bowl has vanished!

coin in the box ★★

a really puzzling recovery of a vanished coin,
and it can be done close up

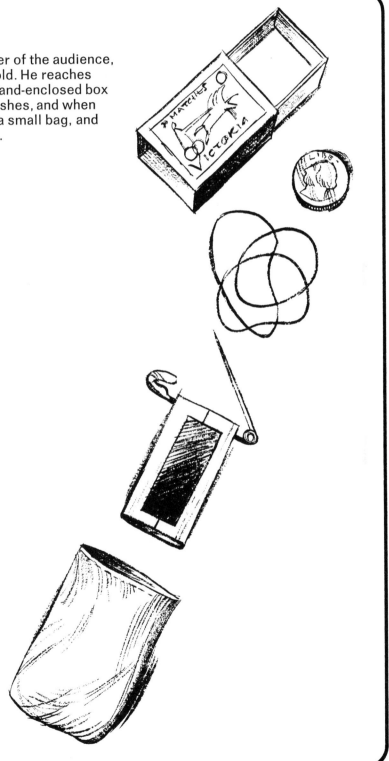

the effect

The magician borrows a quarter from a member of the audience,
has it marked, and gives it to a spectator to hold. He reaches
into his pocket and removes a small, rubber-band-enclosed box
which a second spectator holds. The coin vanishes, and when
the second spectator opens the box, he finds a small bag, and
within it the previously vanished marked coin.

to prepare

Carefully cut apart and flatten
out an aluminum can. Cut out a
2¾-by-3-inch section and bend
it into a 3-inch-long flattened
tube through which a quarter
will slide freely. Tape the tube
shut with plastic electrician's
tape. Glue on (5-Minute epoxy)
a safety pin as illustrated.

Make a small cloth bag just wide
enough for the tube to fit into,
and about 2 inches long.

Obtain a small matchbox and a
number of small rubber bands.

Set the tube into the bag and place the bag into the box as illustrated.

Place the prepared box into your pocket and carefully pin the tube to your jacket lining.

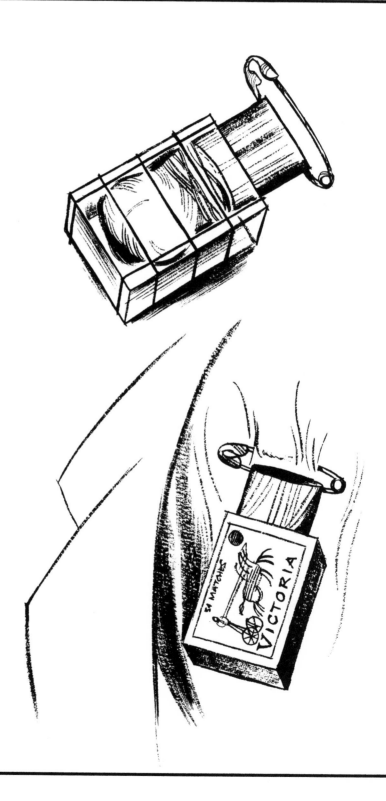

to perform

Borrow a quarter from a member of your audience and have it initialed with a China marking pencil.

Fold the quarter into a sheet of paper (see Paper Fold Vanish, page 134).

Openly reach into your pocket, quickly drop the palmed quarter into the tube, remove the box and hand it to a spectator.

Snap your fingers, tear up the paper and show that the quarter has vanished!

Ask the spectator to open the box he is holding.

The spectator removes the rubber bands, opens the box and the bag, and finds the marked coin within it!

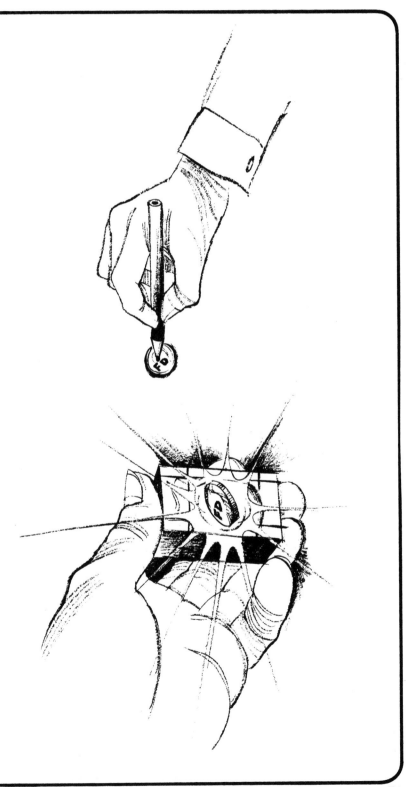

card magic

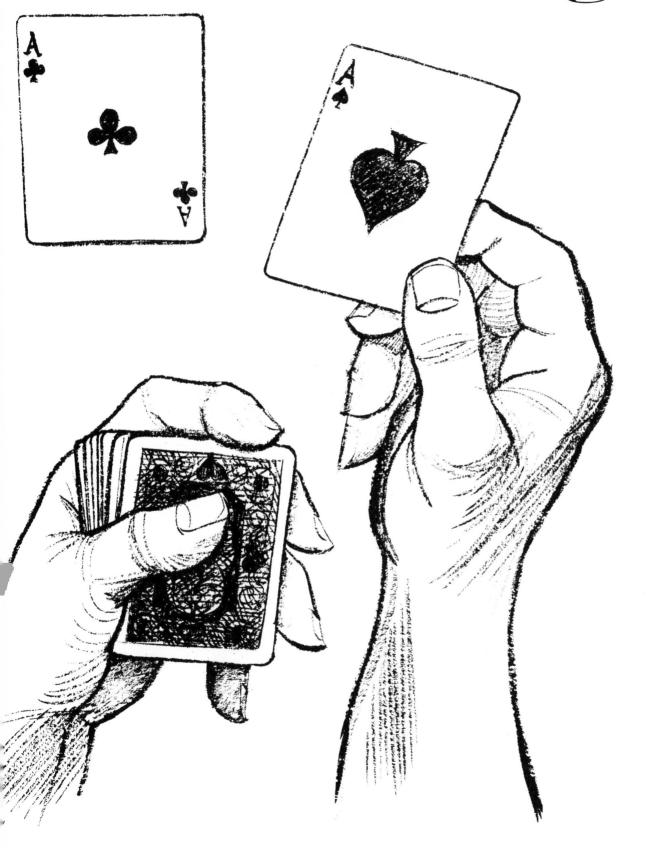

you do as I do ★

*one of the great classics
of card magic, and self-
working too*

the effect

The magician and a spectator each select a card from their own
deck. At the count of three each turns his chosen card over, and
amazingly enough the cards are identical!

to perform

This effect may be performed impromptu or onstage as part of
your act if you like.

Ask a volunteer to assist you. Your patter should sound
something like this:

"I have two decks of cards. I'd like you to select one of them.
Please take either deck. You have a perfectly free choice."

Allow the volunteer to select either pack.

"Now, during this trick you and I are going to do precisely the
same things. First we are each going to shuffle our decks.
You and your helper each shuffle your own deck.

"Fine. Are you satisfied that your deck is thoroughly shuffled?
Good. Let's exchange decks."

As you hand your deck to the spectator secretly glimpse the
bottom card and remember it. That's your *key card.*

"Now you do precisely as I do. Nothing more and nothing less.
Let's open our deck and select a card . . . Take your time, and be
sure not to let me see the card you select, and I won't let you
see mine."

You each thumb through your respective decks and select a card.

"Okay. Now let's close up our decks and place them face-down
on our left palm [or the table if you are close to one], and let's
place each our selected card on top of our own deck.

"Now let's cut the cards. That's right. Cut your selected card
right into the middle of your deck just as I am doing with my
selected card."

You each cut your deck, burying the selected card in the middle.

"Now let's square up our decks so that the selected cards are
completely lost in the deck, and let's cut them a few more times
just to be sure.

"Okay. Now I selected a card from my deck and I cut it somewhere into the pack. You selected a card from your deck and you've cut it somewhere into your pack. Neither one of us could possibly know what card the other selected. Right?

"Now I am going to take your deck and you are going to take mine."

Exchange decks.

"I am going to look through your pack and find the card that I selected and you look through my pack and find the card you selected, but don't let me see your card."

The spectator thumbs through your deck and finds the card he selected, but you ignore the card you selected. Instead thumb through his pack until you locate the key card (the bottom card you secretly glimpsed.) The card to the right of the key card is the one the spectator selected, and this is the card you remove.

"Okay, I found the card I selected. Have you found your card?"

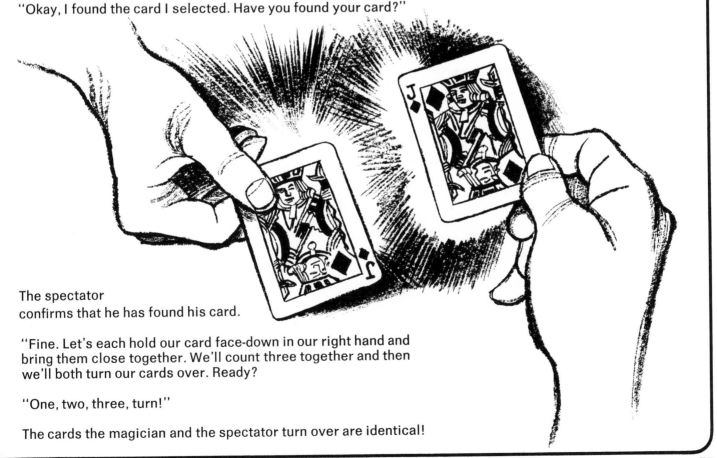

The spectator
confirms that he has found his card.

"Fine. Let's each hold our card face-down in our right hand and bring them close together. We'll count three together and then we'll both turn our cards over. Ready?

"One, two, three, turn!"

The cards the magician and the spectator turn over are identical!

the rising cards ★★★

the great card mystery of all time

the effect

Three cards are selected by three members of the audience and thoroughly shuffled back into the deck, which is placed in an ordinary drinking tumbler that reposes on the magician's table. The selected cards slowly rise up out of the pack one at a time.

NOTE: There are a great many versions of the rising card trick. In *Greater Magic*, John Northern Hilliard describes fifteen methods, and I am sure he has barely scratched the surface. Actually the possibilities range from an impromptu version where the selected card is brought to the top and the pinky, secretly extended, does the deed for you, to a complex and ingenious mechanical device called the Newhart reel (no longer available) that enables any card called for to rise from the deck.

The first version, which follows, is a practical, workable and effective method for accomplishing the basic rising effect. Its weakness is the fact that the magician is obviously aware of the identity of the cards before they rise. Try it first, however.

to prepare

Obtain a glass tumbler with perfectly straight sides into which a full deck of cards will fit. They are not that easy to find, so when you do discover them, get a couple for reserves.

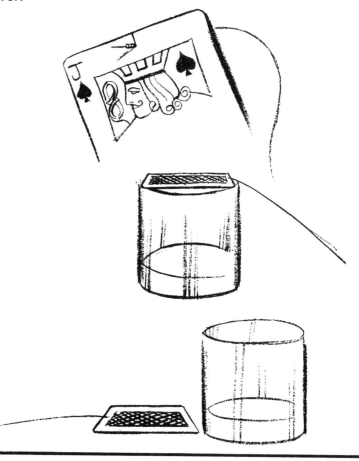

You will also need a length of very fine black silk or nylon thread, a deck of cards and a small tray.

Cut a tiny slit in one end of a playing card. Tie several knots, one on top of the other, in your thread, cut off the surplus as close to the knots as you can, and insert in the slit as illustrated.

Place the prepared card on top of the tumbler, carefully lay the thread on your table so that it won't tangle, and fasten the end of it to the rear of your table with a small tack. If your table is of normal height, the prepared card will be virtually invisible. Try it and see.

If your audience is going to be fairly close or onstage at any point, lay the prepared card flat on your table instead, and keep it hidden behind a crumpled-up silk or some other object you use during your act.

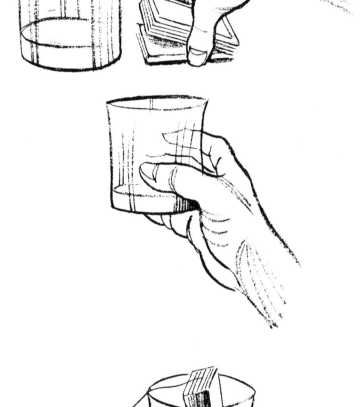

to perform

Show an ordinary deck of cards, have it shuffled by a member of your audience, and allow three cards to be selected and retained. Return to your table, give the deck a brief overhand shuffle, backs to the audience, and lay it down directly on top of the face-down threaded card.

Show the glass to be unmistakably ordinary and allow it to be examined if you like.

Pick up the deck, including the threaded card, and place it in the tumbler so that the thread comes up behind the first card and over the top of the rest of the deck.

Go into your audience and gather the three selected cards on a small tray.

Return to your table and openly insert the first card in the deck about ten or fifteen cards from the front, insert the second card about ten or fifteen cards behind it, and do the same with the third card.

Pick up the tumbler in your left hand and slowly advance towards your audience; the thread will become taut and the chosen cards will rise, one by one, from the deck.

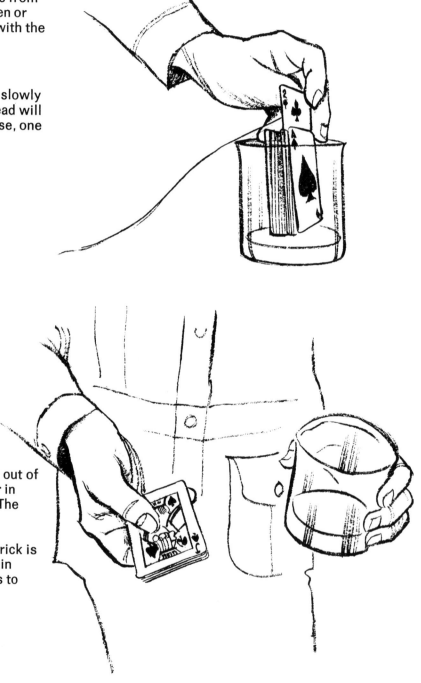

Remove the deck, allow the thread to pull out of the slit in the first card, show the tumbler in your left hand and the deck in your right. The thread, unnoticed, lies on the table.

That, in essence, is the rising cards. The trick is more dramatic if the selected cards remain unknown to the magician, which brings us to

version two

Slit and prepare a card as in the first version and position three cards—say, the ace of hearts, the three of spades and the queen of diamonds—between three indifferent cards as illustrated. These cards are placed face-down on the table as before.

Force (see No-Skill Card Force, page 106) a duplicate ace of hearts, three of spades and queen of diamonds on three members of your audience. Have them shown to other members of the audience (but not to you), and shuffled back into the deck.

Return to your table, place the deck face-down on top of the prepared cards, exhibit the tumbler, and have it examined if you like.

Place the deck, prepared cards and all, into the tumbler and cause the cards, the identity of which you are apparently unaware of, to rise from the deck.

the four aces ★

*the easiest of the four-ace tricks,
but an absolute miracle — when you're lucky!*

the effect

The magician places four aces in a line on the table. He places three indifferent cards on top of each, gathers up the cards, cuts them and allows his audience to do the same as often as they like. He then deals the cards into four piles and asks someone to point to any pile. That pile is turned over and found to contain the four aces!

to perform

Openly thumb through the deck, remove the four aces and place them on the bottom of the pack as you say: "We need the four aces for this trick. Here they are."

Deal the four aces face-up in a row from left to right.

"One, two, three, four. Now we deal three indifferent cards on top of each ace. Watch closely."

Turn the aces face-down, and turning the deck face-down in the left hand, deal three indifferent cards, one at a time from left to right, on top of each ace. "One, two, three, four, one, two, three, four, one, two, three, four."

Lay the balance of the deck aside, well away from the four piles.

"We place the rest of the cards over here where we can't get at them. Now we gather up the piles, keeping the aces at the bottom of each."

Gather up the piles, one at a time, in the left hand, starting with the left pile. Place the one large pile face-down on the table, and square it up.

"Okay. We have four aces and three indifferent cards on top of each. Naturally if we were to lay out the cards again, all of the aces would appear in the fourth pile, so to prevent that from happening, we're going to cut the cards."

Make a single cut and complete the cut.

"In fact, we'll do it a couple of more times just to mix them up."

Cut the cards again, complete the cut, and repeat once or twice more.

"Would you do the same thing, please? Just cut the cards and complete the cut. Cut them again. In fact, cut them as often as you like."

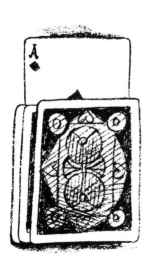   

Don't allow anyone to shuffle or to otherwise mix the cards. The cards must be cut once and then the cut must be completed; this may be repeated any number of times.

"Okay. Are you satisfied that the cards are thoroughly mixed up?"

If your audience agrees, then proceed. If not, allow them to cut the cards again.

"Okay. Now let's lay the cards out again. One, two, three, four. One, two, three, four. One, two, three, four. One, two, three, four. Now by this time you know the aces have to be pretty thoroughly mixed up."

Look at one person and address your remarks to him or her.

"Would you concentrate on one pile? Point to the pile you are thinking about, please."

The person points to that pile.

"Okay. Watch . . ."

Turn over the selected pile.

If by lucky coincidence it happens to contain the four aces, say with great emphasis, "Amazing! The pile you pointed to—the pile of your choice— contains the four aces!"

As you quickly turn over the other piles one by one to show the indifferent cards, take your bows. You have just performed a miracle!

Of course the chances are only one in four that the aces will actually be in the first pile chosen.

More than likely, that pile will contain four indifferent cards. If that happens, you say, "Note that none of the four aces are in the pile you pointed to. That means they must be mixed up in the other three piles. Would you point to another pile, please."

If the next pile contains the four aces, you simply say, "Despite the thoroughness with which we have mixed the cards, all four aces have gathered together in one pile," and you have performed a good trick.

If, however, that pile did not contain the four aces, you still have a good chance to pull off that miracle, in which case you push that pile aside, and again say, "None of the aces are in this pile, either, which means that they have to be mixed up in the remaining two piles. Will you please point to one of them."

At this point you have a fifty-fifty chance for success. If the third choice does contain the aces you say, "Despite the thoroughness with which we mixed the cards, all four aces have gathered together in one pile."

If, hopefully, that pile does not contain the four aces, you pounce on the opportunity and say, "Notice that none of the four aces are here. Miraculously enough, the aces have gathered into the last pile, the pile you have chosen by the process of elimination!"

an alternate method

If the aces had small, secret marks on the back, or if you were to look at the face of the first few cards after they were cut, you would quickly know which pile the aces would fall in and then you could force your audience to choose the correct pile. In this method the spectator always selects the pile with the aces; however, the effect isn't quite as spectacular as the first method when it works right.

to perform

After the cards have been cut to your audience's satisfaction, casually and quickly glance at the faces of the first few cards as you say, "They're mixed, all right."

The position of the ace will tell you which pile the aces will appear in. If the first card is an ace, all the aces will be in the first pile. If the second card is an ace, all the aces will appear in the second pile, and so on. Now your problem is to force the ace pile on your audience.

Deal out the four piles as in the first method, and say, "Please point to any two piles."

If one of the two chosen piles contains the aces, say, "Fine."

Push aside the two other piles.

If the ace pile is not in one of the two chosen piles, say, "Fine. That leaves these two piles."

Push aside the two chosen piles. In either case, one of the two piles remaining on the table contains the aces, and you know which one it is. Say, "Please point to one of the remaining piles."

If the spectator points to the pile that contains the aces, you flick the other pile away and say, "Amazing! The pile of your choice contains the four aces!"

If they point to the pile that does not contain the four aces, you flick that one aside and with equal enthusiasm you say, "Amazing! The pile of your choice contains the four aces!"

NOTE: As you gain experience with this trick, you will find it increasingly easy to influence the spectator's choice by placing the ace pile a trifle forward of the other piles or by dealing the aces at a slight angle when the other piles are straight. Try it and see.

Incidentally, I find that in the great majority of cases the audience selects the third pile counting from your left.

reverso★★

a quick trick by a brilliant Japanese magician, the late Tenkai

the effect

The magician very obviously reverses half of the cards, but when he taps the deck, all the cards mysteriously right themselves.

to prepare

Reverse the bottom card of the deck.

to perform

1 Cut off the top portion of the deck.

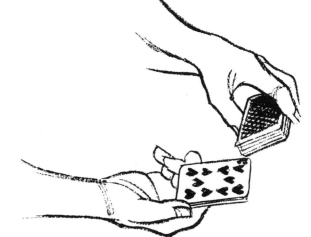

2 Openly reverse that portion, and as you do, secretly turn over the portion remaining in your left hand.

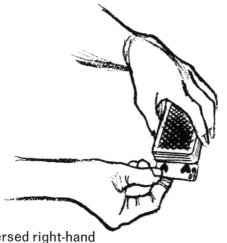

3 Place the reversed right-hand portion on the bottom of the left-hand portion.

4 Push the cards flush.

5 Turn the deck end over end once
6 and twice and three times.

7 Pull off the top card and insert it anywhere into the deck.

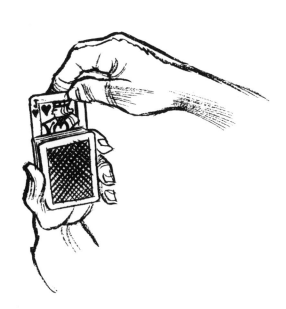

8 Pull off the bottom card, reverse it, and insert it anywhere into the deck.

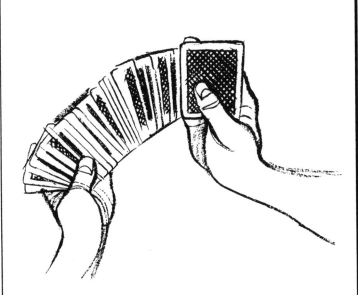

9 Tap the deck and spread to show that all the cards have righted themselves.

the lazy location ★

a sure-fire quickie by
U. F. Grant

the effect

The magician has a card selected and replaced in the deck. He announces that rather than go to the trouble of finding the card himself, he will magically cause a card in the deck to turn over and find the selected card for him, and that's exactly what happens.

to prepare

Find a six-spot, reverse it, and place it sixth from the bottom of the deck.

to perform

Have someone select a card, look at it, show it to the others and place it on top of the deck.

Cut about half the cards from the bottom of the deck, throw them on top of the selected card and square the deck.

Then say, "Of course I could find your card, but this time I'm going to do it the easy way. I'm going to snap my fingers, and when I do, one of the cards in the deck is going to reverse itself and tell us where your card is."

Spread the deck until you come to the reversed card, and say, "The six of diamonds [or whatever]! Okay, let's see what it's trying to tell us."

Starting with the card beneath the reversed six, count, "One, two, three, four, five and the sixth card . . ."

Turn over the sixth card.

". . . is your card—the nine of clubs [or whatever]."

muscle reading ★

*a dynamite effect and
incredibly easy to do*

to perform

Say, "Shuffle the deck. Do a thorough job, and whenever you are ready, hand me the cards."

As you take the cards, secretly glimpse the bottom card and remember it. That is your "key card." If you can't get a glimpse without being detected, give the deck a quick overhand shuffle yourself and peek at that point.

"Now to convince you beyond a shadow of a doubt that I don't sneak looks at any of the cards, I'm going to turn around, hold the cards behind my back, and ask you to select one. You have a perfectly free choice."

Place the cards behind your back, turn around and spread the cards for the spectator's selection.

As soon as a card is chosen, say, "Okay, look at your card, remember it and place it on top of the deck."

The spectator replaces the card on top of the deck, and with the cards still behind your back, cut off the bottom portion of the deck and place it on the top, thus burying the spectator's card. (The selected card is now underneath your "key card.")

Bring the cards from behind your back, place them on the table, cut them and invite the spectator to do the same. Then ribbon-spread the cards face-up on the table, saying, "We are going to use an interesting method to try to locate your card. It is called muscle reading. Notice that I said 'try' to find your card. I am not at all sure I can, but let's take a crack at it anyway and see what happens. Please hold my right wrist lightly and mentally will me to your card."

The spectator holds your wrist as you extend your forefinger and slowly pass your hand over the spread cards.

As soon as you spot the key card you know that the selected card is immediately to its right. Hesitate at this point, waver back and forth, touch the card next to the selected card, and finally push the selected card forward.

"Was that your card?"

The spectator, with an astonished look in his face, says yes.

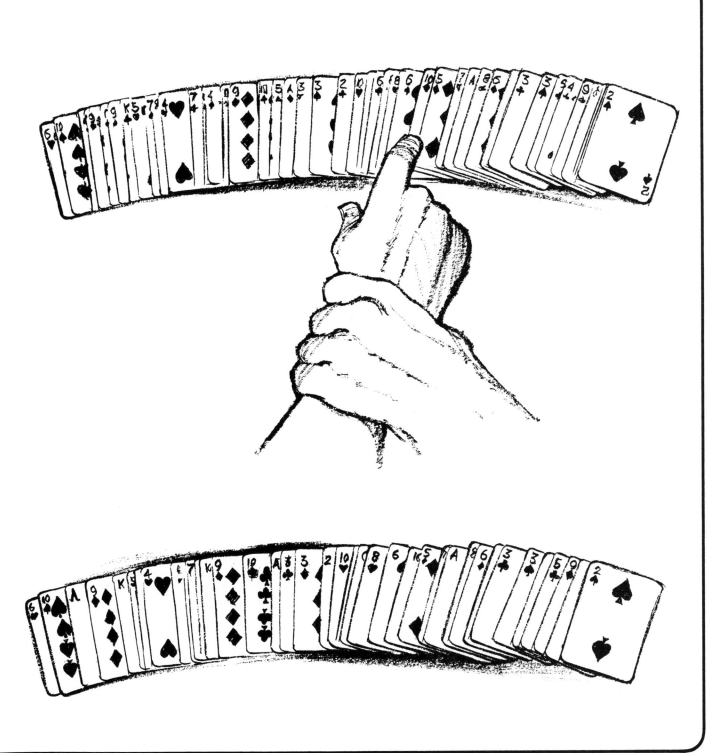

you're the magician★★

a clever trick where the spectator unwittingly locates his own card

the effect

A spectator selects a card, buries it in the deck and places the deck behind his back. He then turns a card upside-down and plunges it into the deck. When he spreads the cards he discovers that the upside-down card is directly above the card he previously selected.

to perform

Ask a spectator to assist you. Say, "You're going to be the magician. Take the deck and shuffle it as thoroughly as you like.

"Now square up the cards and place them on my palm. Take about half the deck. I'll keep the half you left and place it behind my back so that I can't see any of the cards.

"Thumb through your half and select any card you like. Take your time. You have a perfectly free choice. Show your card to everybody, but don't let me see it.

"Place your selected card face-down on the top of your half of the deck, square up your cards and hold them face-down on your palm."

While this has been going on, you quietly (behind your back) reverse the bottom card of your half of the deck so that it is now face-up. Do the same thing with the second card from the top of your pack.

Square up your cards and place your pack on top of the spectator's pack. Unbeknownst to him, a reversed card is now directly over his selected card.

"Okay. Place the pack behind your back and do exactly what I tell you.

"Place the top card of the deck on the bottom.

"Now reverse the next card. Turn it face-up and insert it somewhere into the middle of the deck. Okay?

"Now let's see what kind of a magician you are. I'm not even going to touch the cards. You're going to do it all! Thumb through the pack until you come to the card you reversed.

"There it is. Now what was the name of the card you selected?"

The spectator names his card.

"Look at the next card—the card immediately underneath the card you reversed in the deck."

The spectator turns over the next card.

"There it is! The four of diamonds [or whatever]. Congratulations. You're a fine magician!"

the twentieth card ★

a real puzzler and very
quick and easy to do

the effect

The spectator looks through the deck and selects
a card, and the magician, without knowing what it
is, magically makes it appear as the twentieth
card in the deck.

to perform

Ask a spectator to help you do the trick. Say,
"I'd like you to examine the deck and then shuffle
it as thoroughly as you like.

"Now please think of a number between one and
ten, but don't tell me what it is. Count down to
that number from the top of the deck, note the
card at that number, but don't remove it. Just
remember what it is. I'll turn away while you are
doing it so that I can't see the card."

The spectator counts down to the number he
thought of, notes the card and leaves it at that
position.

"Okay. May I have the deck, please?"

You take the deck from the spectator, hold it
behind your back and rapidly count off twenty
cards from the top, reversing their order as you
do so, and then replacing them on the top of the
deck. As you do this, say, "You thought of a
number. You looked at the card that was at that
number and you did it all while my back was
turned.

"Despite the fact that there is no way in the
world for me to know what card you selected or
where in the deck it is, I am going to make your
card the twentieth in the deck."

Bring the deck in front of you and ask the
spectator what number he thought of. Count out
loud, one card for each number, starting the count
with the spectator's number.

If his number was five, for example, count the first card as five, the next as six, and so on until you reach twenty.

"What was the number you thought of? Five [or whatever]? Okay. Watch closely. We count from the top of the deck, starting with number five, six, seven, eight . . . twenty. This is the twentieth card. Name your card, please."

As he names his card you turn it over, and sure enough, it's the one he named!

NOTE: I find it difficult to talk and count to twenty behind my back at the same time. I count to five four times. If you have the same problem, try this method.

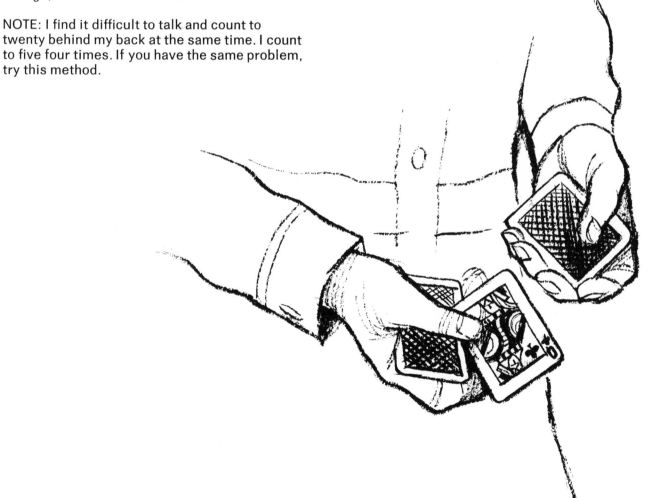

double reverse ★★

*a real gem by a great card
man, the late Nate Leipzig*

the effect

The magician invites a spectator to take half the
deck while he retains the other half. They each
select a card from their own portions and,
without divulging it, insert it in the other's half.
The deck is then reunited, the cards are fanned
out, and two cards are seen to be reversed. One
is the spectator's, the other is the magician's!

to prepare

Secretly reverse and memorize the bottom card
on the deck.

to perform

Hold the deck face-down on your left palm and
invite a spectator to cut off approximately half
the deck.

Say, "Please thumb through your cards and select
one, but don't let me see it. I'll do the same with
my half of the deck.

"Okay, now let's each place our cards face-down
on our left palms like this . . . Now I'm going to
put my card in your half of the pack . . ."

Reach over and place your card, face-down, into
the spectator's half of the deck. As you do so,
drop your left hand naturally to your side, and
immediately reverse the pack so that they all
are face-up on your palm except for the now top
card, which is face-down. Bring your arm up
again.

". . . and I'd like you to place your card face-
down in my half, but don't let me see it . . ."

Hold the cards loosely, but do not spread them.
I generally riffle one corner slightly to facilitate
the entry of the spectator's card.

"Please cut your portion of the cards one time and
replace the cut . . ."

As the spectator does so, again drop your left hand to your side and reverse your pack.

"...and I'll do the same."

Cut your portion once.

"Now place your half of the deck on mine and cut them once more."

The spectator places his cards on yours, cuts the deck and completes the cut.

"Good. Now watch me very closely. Nothing slick or tricky."

The deck is still on your outstretched left hand.

"I selected the _____ of _____ [name the card that you reversed on the bottom of the deck]. What was the card that you selected?"

The spectator names his card.

"Watch. Only two cards in the deck reversed..."

Spread the cards so that the two reversed cards are clearly visible.

"...the _____ of _____ that I selected, and the _____ of _____ that you selected!"

the telltale card ★

*a strong trick your
audience will love*

the effect

The initials of the chosen card mysteriously
appear on the spectator's wrist!

to prepare

Use a very soft lead pencil to write the initials
of a card—say, the seven of hearts (7H)—on a
cube of sugar and place it in your right jacket
pocket, initial side up.

Place the seven of hearts in the deck as indicated
in No-Skill Card Force (page 106).

to perform

Force the seven of hearts. As the spectator takes
the card and shows it to the audience, casually
place your right hand in your jacket pocket, place
the ball of your thumb on the initials and press
hard, thus transferring them from the sugar to
your thumb.

Ask the spectator to place his left hand palm-up
and parallel with the floor, and to place the
selected card face-down on it.

Grasp his left wrist with your right hand, your
thumb on top at the base of his hand, thus passing
the initial to his wrist.

At the same time, grasp his right wrist with your
left in the same manner, turn his hand over and
place it palm-down on top of the card.

Say words to the effect that "some cards have a
strong life-force of their own—so strong, in fact,
that they are sometimes capable of making their
identity known in very strange and mysterious
ways.

"Let's see whether that's true in this case. Do
you feel anything?"

Remove your right hand. "What's that by your
hand? The seven of hearts! Is that the card you
selected? You see, some cards do have a life-
force of their own!"

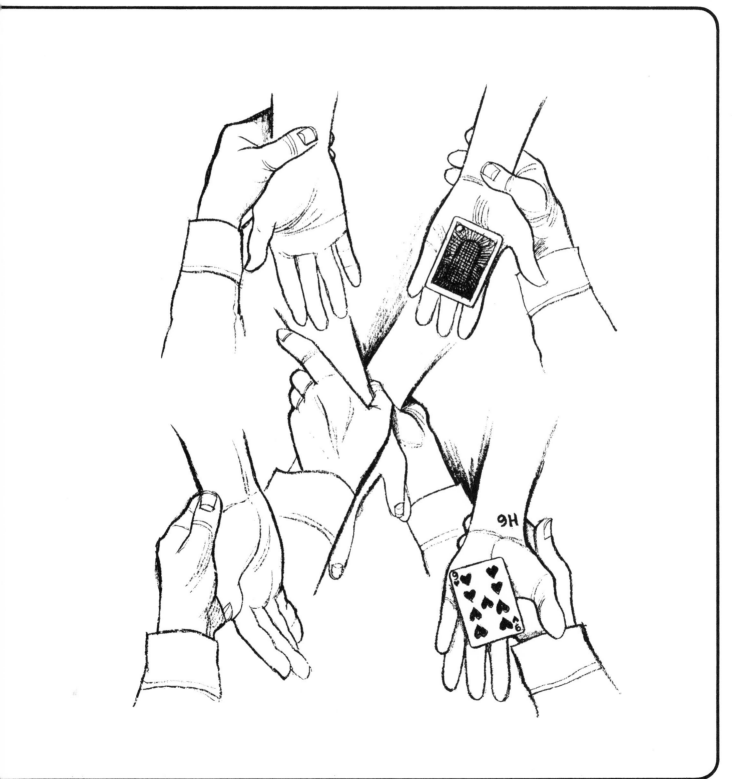

one-way deck principle

One of the most widely known card location techniques is called the one-way principle.

A one-way deck—as you are probably aware—is one in which the pattern of the cards are not identical when viewed from either end.

If all the cards are arranged with the pattern running one way, and a card is reversed, end for end, in the deck, that card can be easily detected simply by glancing at the backs of the cards.

Of course most one-way patterns—bridge decks in particular—are painfully obvious, particularly to anyone even vaguely aware of the principle. Certain poker-sized decks, however, are so indetectably one-way as to be totally above suspicion. Following are a couple that are excellent, but not too easy to find:

Rider backs   Small curl and a dot on upper left hand corner. No dot on diagonally opposite corner.

Wheel backs   Position of the third wing makes this one-way pattern obvious.

If you like, you can make your own one-way patterns. A dot of red or blue ink hidden in the pattern at one end of each card will convert your deck very effectively.

think "stop" ★

*a great trick, the original version
of which was invented by the late Al Baker*

the effect

A card is freely selected and returned to the deck, which is cut several times. The magician requests the spectator to think "stop" when he sees his card. He then turns the cards face-up one at a time, and without any visible signal from the spectator, he automatically stops the instant the selected card appears.

to prepare

Set the deck up one-way.

to perform

Give the deck a thorough overhand shuffle and allow a spectator to select any card.

Reverse the deck, end for end, and have the selected card returned. Say, "You've selected a card, you've returned it, and now it's lost somewhere in the deck, and since I haven't the vaguest idea where, I'd like you to help me find it.

"I'm going to turn the cards face-up one at a time. When your card comes up, don't give me any indication that you have seen it. Instead, think 'stop' to yourself as hard as you can, and we'll see if I can pick up your mental command. Okay?"

Turn the cards face-up one at a time. When you spot the selected card, which is reversed end for end, you turn it up, stop and say, "I think I have just gotten your message to stop. Is this your card, the _____ of _____?"

elimination ★

a surprisingly effective trick

to prepare

Reverse one card, end for end, in a one-way
deck and remember it.

to perform

Openly write the name of the reversed card on a
slip of paper, fold it, seal it in an envelope if
you like, and give it to someone to hold.

Pick up the deck, and as you give it an overhand
shuffle say, "I've just made a prediction. Now
we're going to try a little experiment and see how
accurate I've been. I'm going to place the cards
down on the table, and I'm not going to touch
them from this point on. You're going to do all
the work.

"Pick up the deck, cut it, and replace the cut. Cut it a few more times if you like. It's entirely up to you.

"Okay, now deal the deck into four face-down piles."

Watch the back of the cards and note which pile the reversed card falls in.

When the cards are all dealt out, say, "Okay. Let's eliminate some cards . . . Let's see, shall we push that pile aside? And, unh, how about that one? . . . And let's eliminate that one too."

In an apparently haphazard fashion, have your helper push aside all the piles but the one that contains the predicted card.

"Now deal the remaining cards into four face-down piles."

Your helper deals the remaining cards into four smaller piles, and you note where the predicted card falls.

"Point to two of the piles."

If one of the two selected piles contains the predicted card, have your helper retain those and push the other two aside.

If they do not contain the predicted card, have them eliminated and retain the other two, saying, "Okay. Now point to one of the two remaining piles."

Using the same method, have the pile which contains the predicted card retained and have the three or four cards it contains dealt out on the table.

Repeat the same process of elimination so that only the predicted card remains.

Have the prediction read and ask your helper to turn over the remaining card.

It and the predicted card are one!

the impossible location ★

a real card miracle

the effect

The magician asks a spectator to shuffle the deck. He takes the mixed deck, cuts it into two piles and turns away while the spectator selects one card from either pile and buries it in the other. The magician then shuffles the piles together and passes five or six cards at a time in front of the spectator with the request that the spectator give absolutely no indication when or if he sees his card. After a number of cards have been passed the magician reveals the spectator's card.

to prepare

Set the deck up one-way.

to perform

Ask the spectator to give the deck a thorough shuffle "like this" and indicate an overhand shuffle. (A riffle shuffle might destroy the one-way setup.)

When he is finished, ask him to set the deck down on the table, and say, "Let's cut the deck into two piles."

Cut the cards and place the left-hand portion to the left and the right-hand portion to the right as illustrated. One-half of the deck is now facing one way and one-half is facing the other.

"I'm going to turn around so that I can't possibly see anything you do.

"Now while my back is turned, please take any card you like from either half of the deck and bury it somewhere in the other half. Then place either half on the other, square the cards, and let me know when you are finished.

"I'm going to pass certain groups of cards in front of you. If you happen to see your card, please don't say anything or indicate in any way that you have seen your card."

Pass the cards in front of the spectator in groups of five or six and then place each group down on the table.

When you spot the reversed card, place that group down as well. Hesitate, and then say, "I have a strange feeling that we may have just passed your card."

Reach down, pick up the selected card, and turn it over as you say, "Was your card the _____ of _____?"

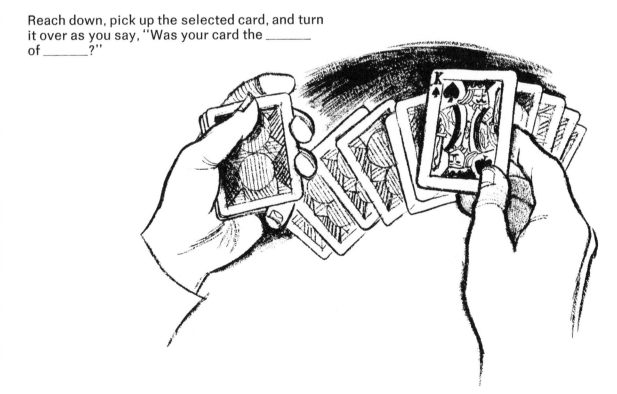

on forcing

Forcing is the technique by which you appear to give a spectator a free choice but actually induce him to select the object you want him to have. This can be accomplished in any one of a number of ways. If you are an accomplished magician, the problem is academic. In most instances, you can achieve the results you want with sleight of hand. If you are not, then of course you have to depend on mechanical or self-working methods to help you along. Following are a few that work well.

the forcing deck

The easiest way to force a single card is by use of a forcing deck. You pick up your deck, give it a shuffle or two and ask someone to select a card. They do and invariably select the card you want them to select. Why? Because all fifty-two cards in the deck are nines of clubs or sevens of hearts or whatever.

Suppose you had to force three cards (see Rising Cards, page 76)? Simple enough. You would use a three-way forcing deck. The first third of the deck would consist of seventeen of the first card you wanted to force, the second third would consist of seventeen of the second card to be forced, and the last would contain seventeen of the third card to be forced.

Your problem is to induce each of three individuals selecting a card to do so from the appropriate portion of the deck.

A more subtle method would be to prearrange the deck so that the three cards appear in the same sequence throughout—AD, 3H, JS, AD, 3H, JS, AD, 3H, JS, and so on.

You place the cards face-down on a small tray and ask someone to cut them a few times (single cuts only, each of which must be completed). You then request a spectator to cut the cards and select the top card of the cut portion, ask a second person to take the next card and a third to take the one after that.

In one of his superb books on advanced techniques for accomplished magicians, Frank Garcia, who is certainly one of a handful of top sleight-of-hand men in the whole world, explains an ingenious forcing technique used by European card men.

Beforehand, place the card to be forced seventh from the top of the deck. Ask a spectator to give you a number *between* five and ten.

If the number is six, deal two cards at a time on the table and ask the spectator to take the next card, which is the force card.

If the number is seven, repeat the procedure outlined above.

If the number is eight, deal by twos and have the spectator take the top (eighth) card on the pile, which will be the force card.

If the number is nine, count in groups of three and have the spectator take the top (ninth) card on the pile, which will be the force card.

no-skill card force

an easy, super-effective
way to force a card

the effect

In a great many card tricks the magician must "force" a particular card on a spectator. In this self-working method the spectator is asked to call out any number between one and twenty. The magician counts down to the freely selected number and asks the spectator to look at the card at that number. The "freely selected" card happens to be the card the magician "forced."

to prepare

Place the card you want to force—say, the three of hearts—third from the top of the deck.

to perform

If you can, very casually give the deck a quick riffle shuffle, keeping the top three cards intact.

Say, "I'd like someone to call out a number between one and twenty. You, sir? Fine. Any number between one and twenty. You have a free choice."

Assume the number called is twelve.

"Twelve? Okay. One, two, three [and so forth]."

Quickly count one card for each number face-down to fourteen, appear momentarily confused, and say, "Wait a minute, what was the number? Twelve, right? I'm sorry. Let's try that again."

Toss the cards you counted back on top of the deck, and count down, one card per number, to twelve.* Push the twelfth card slightly forward.

"Okay. There's the card you wanted. Please look at it, show it to the others, but don't let me see it."

At this point you have the card, which you know to be the three of hearts, either replaced in the deck, held, or whatever the trick you are doing calls for.

* Always count two more than the number selected.

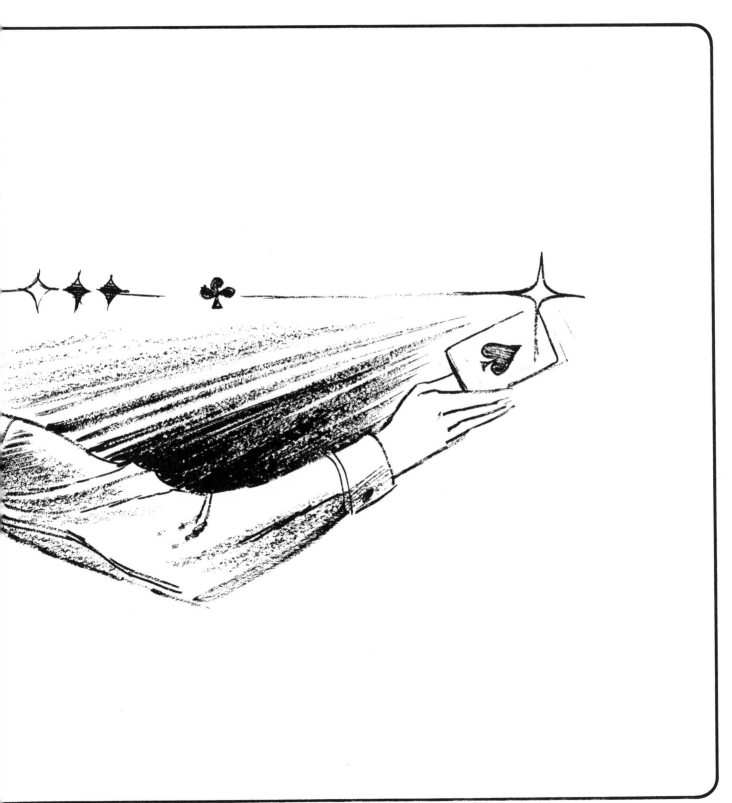

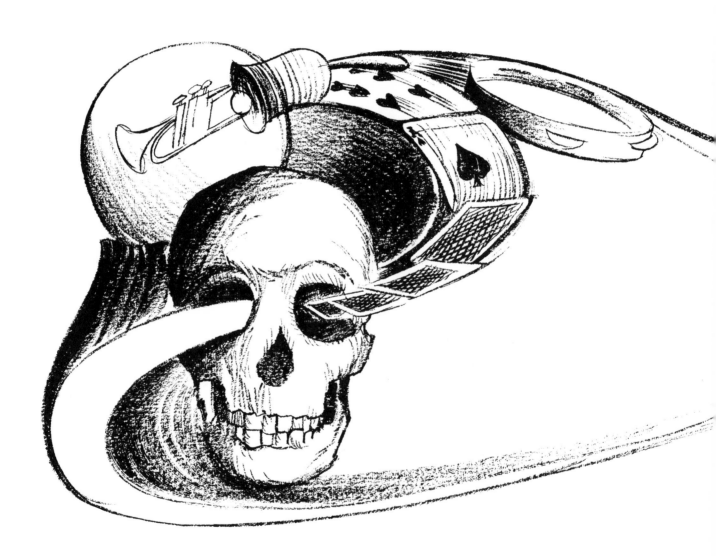

mental magic

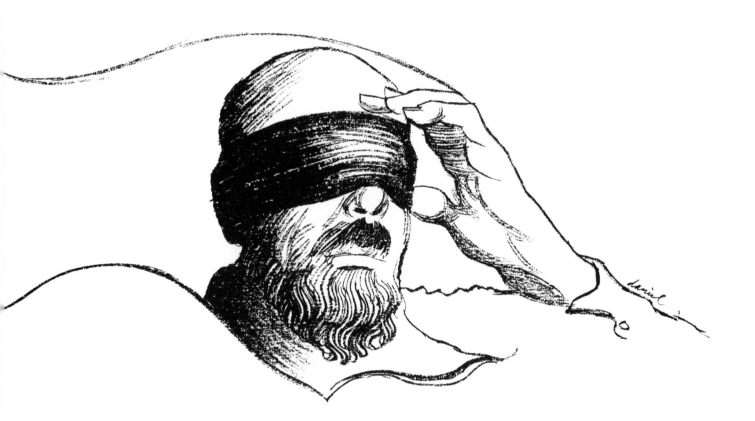

second sight with cards ★★

an easy two-person code
that fools them every time

the effect

The magician allows various persons to select
cards from an unprepared deck. His partner, the
"medium," seated some distance away,
immediately names the cards selected.

to prepare

You and your partner must memorize the
following code. Learn it to absolute perfection
and practice it well before using it in a trick.

code for the suits

Hearts—(say nothing)	Clubs—now
Diamonds—just	Spades—okay *or* all right

code for the values

Ace—remember	8—look-see
2—don't	9—try
3—hold	10—think
4—concentrate	Jack—picture
5—place	Queen—name
6—say	King—project *or* send
7—keep	

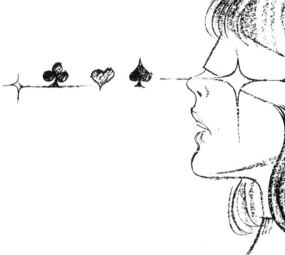
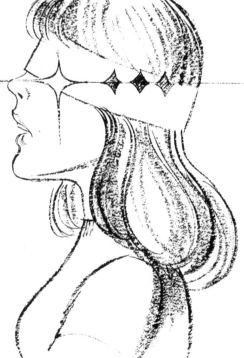

to perform

Speak briefly about telepathy and then offer to give a demonstration.

If this act is performed impromptu, your medium can be seated anywhere in the room provided he or she cannot see the cards that are selected. If you are working on a stage, you might have him or her blindfolded and seated on a chair at center stage.

Shuffle a deck, go out into your audience, and holding the cards face-up, thumb through them and invite spectators to point to cards.

Do not address the medium. Speak only to the person who selected a card.

Assume, for example, that the three of clubs was the card chosen. Say, "*Now hold* your finger on your card for a moment."

The first two words you utter tell the medium what the card is. *Now* designates clubs and *hold* designates three.

The medium says, "I get an impression of the three of clubs."

Of course you could have said anything as long as *now hold* were the first two words. For example, "*Now hold* everything and let's see if she gets your card." Or "*Now hold* the image of the card in your mind."

numbers, numbers ★

*a puzzling effect and easier
than most number tricks*

to perform

Ask a member of your audience—preferably
someone you have never met before or don't
know too well—to jot down the last four digits
of his telephone number.

Tell him to transpose or alter the order of those
same four digits any way that he likes and jot
the new number down.

Have him subtract the smaller of the two
numbers from the larger.

He is then to add the digits in the answer
together so that they total one digit. If they total
more than one digit they are to be added together
again until they do add up to a single digit.

Tell the spectator to add 16 to the number he
came up with.

Now ask him to add that number to the last two
digits of his birthdate and to tell you the answer.

Subtract 25 from whatever number the spectator
tells you, and you will have accurately divined
the year of the spectator's birth.

How does it work? Very simple. No matter what
the spectator's telephone number, and regardless
of how he alters the order of that number, the
answer will always come out to 9!

Nine plus 16 equals 25. That number is constant.
Now all you have to do is subtract 25 from the
number he gives you (which is his birth year
plus 25) and you know the year in which he was
born.

$$7453$$
$$-3547$$
$$\overline{3906}$$

$$3 + 9 = 12 + 0 = 12 + 6 = 18$$
$$1 + 8 = 9$$
$$9 + 16 = 25$$

$$19\overline{)35}$$
$$+25$$
$$\overline{60}$$
$$-25$$
$$\overline{35}$$

SPECTATORS BIRTHDATE IS 1935

table divination ★

*an old trick devised by the great
magic writer Walter B. Gibson*

the effect

The magician assembles seven objects and asks a spectator to think of one of them. He taps the objects with a knife and the spectator mentally spells out the name of the object, one letter for each tap. Amazingly enough, the magician's last tap ends on the spectator's object.

to prepare

Memorize the following list in the order given.

cup
fork
plate
napkin
ashtray
matchbox
cigarette

to perform

Assemble the listed objects. You may substitute any other object for one that has the same number of letters—for example, a knife or a glass for a plate, or a saucer for a napkin, and so on.

Say, "I'd like you to watch very closely. I've assembled six . . . one, two, three . . . [count quickly, somewhat to yourself] . . . no, seven objects. I'd like you to think of one of them. Don't tell me what it is. I'm going to take my magic knife [pick up a knife from the table] and tap various objects. I'd like you to spell out, to yourself, one letter of the object you selected for each tap. For example, c . . . u . . . p, or whatever. When you come to the last letter of the object you selected, say 'stop.' Okay?"

Tap any two objects. On your third, tap the cup, your fourth, the fork, and so on down the list. When the spectator says "stop," you will automatically be tapping the object he has mentally selected.

fingers that see ★

*a puzzling and entertaining
little pocket trick*

the effect

The magician passes three different-colored
poker chips to members of his audience. They
examine the chips, select one and hand it to the
magician behind his back. He feels the chip,
accurately divines its color, and repeats his
success several more times.

to prepare

Obtain three different-colored poker chips.

Drill a ¼-inch hole through the middle of each
chip.

Set one chip aside, carefully enlarge the hole in
the second chip with a piece of fine sandpaper
wrapped around a small dowel stick, and enlarge
the hole in the third chip to a slightly greater
degree.

When you are finished each chip should fit on to
the sharpened end of a pencil to a slightly
greater extent than the chip before it.

Secrete the pencil in your back pocket or fasten
it onto a piece of elastic that is pinned inside the
back of your jacket but dangles down close to its
bottom edge so that you can easily obtain it.

to perform

Pass the chips out to members of your audience and request that they hand you any color behind your back. Reach under your jacket, obtain the pencil (or into your back pocket if that is more convenient for you) and fit the sharpened end into the hole.

The depth to which the pencil penetrates tells you the color of the chip.

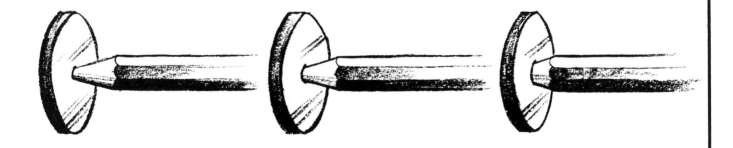

the great telephone trick ★

a stunning trick and a
great reputation-builder

the effect

A borrowed deck is thoroughly shuffled, and
anyone in the audience freely selects a card
from it. That person or anyone else present goes
to the telephone, calls up a friend of the
magician's and asks him to name the selected
card. He does so without hesitation!

to prepare

Prepare two small cards with the following names
and give one to a trusted friend.

Paste the duplicate card into a pocket telephone
address book.

AH	Harris	AD	Daley	AC	Chapman	AS	Sammons
2H	Henslow	2D	Dalton	2C	Cavanagh	2S	Schaefer
3H	Henning	3D	Dahl	3C	Costello	3S	Stevens
4H	Halsey	4D	Daniels	4C	Chanin	4S	Smith
5H	Hartley	5D	Danton	5C	Colson	5S	Scott
6H	Hunter	6D	Dana	6C	Collins	6S	Shuster
7H	Humphrey	7D	Donaldson	7C	Coleman	7S	Scully
8H	Hummel	8D	D'Angelo	8C	Conklin	8S	Scudder
9H	Hughes	9D	Darby	9C	Condon	9S	Seller
10H	Huggens	10D	Davis	10C	Connors	10S	Seward
JH	Hopper	JD	Dean	JC	Cooney	JS	Shelley
QH	Hooper	QD	Decker	QC	Cooper	QS	Shepard
KH	Herman	KD	Delman	KC	Cook	KS	Simons

to perform

Since the use of a telephone is required, this
trick is more conveniently presented in a private
home than it is on a stage or in a club.

Borrow a deck of cards and have one or more
spectators shuffle it.

Set the deck down and ask someone to go
through it, select a card, and show it to everyone
present. Explain that it doesn't matter if you
know the card. (Actually you must know what
card was chosen.)

Your patter should go something like this:

"In this modern era most scientists accept the fact that there are people who are capable of extrasensory perception. For the most part, of course, they can only pick up messages which are transmitted from fairly close range. I know a person, however, who is absolutely extraordinary. He is so sensitively attuned to thought waves that he can actually sense messages from a great distance away. For example, if we were all to concentrate on the card that has just been chosen I think we could actually call him on the telephone and have him name it. Would you like to try?"

Your audience will be excited at the prospect. You casually reach into your pocket and remove your address book, quickly turn to the page where you have pasted in your master list, and look up the appropriate name for the selected card as you say, "I'm not sure I remember his number . . . Oh, yes, here it is—MU 7–9636 [or whatever]."

Put the book back in your pocket, and then, almost as an afterthought, say, "His name is Stevens . . . Anybody . . . Just call MU 7–9636 and ask for Mr. Stevens. Tell him you're a friend of mine and ask him to please try to name the card we are all concentrating on."

As soon as he hears the name "Stevens" your friend checks his list, which he has kept by the phone, discovers that Stevens is the code for the three of spades, and says, "You are thinking of a black card. A spade. The three of spades."

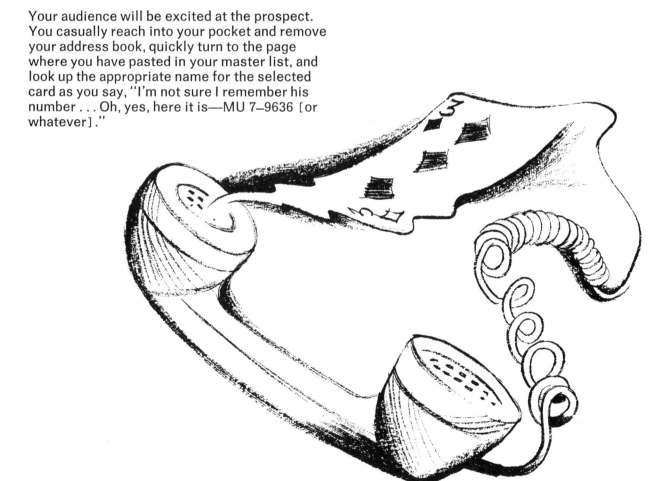

one ahead ★★

an amazingly simple system,
but it has fooled a lot of people

to present

Ask a spectator to thoroughly shuffle a deck of cards and spread the cards out face-down on the table.

Gaze thoughtfully at the cards, touch one somewhat hesitantly, and say, "The six of hearts" (or any other card you like). Pick up the card without letting anyone see it, glance at it briefly and hold it so it can't be seen or place it face-down in front of you on the table.

Immediately repeat the process, but this time as you point to any card on the table, call out the name of the first card you picked up.

Repeat again, calling each card you point to by the name of the one you have just picked up.

After you have named six or seven cards, fan them faces toward you and say, "What were the cards I named? Do you recall?"

The spectators will call off the cards you named, and as they do so, toss that particular card face-up on the table.

If they don't remember each card, and they probably won't, you can refresh their memory by saying, "You remember the seven of clubs. Right? And the nine of hearts?" and so forth.

Of course one card—the first, which is the one you used to start the one-ahead system, will be wrong, but your audience may not remember that, and if they do, six out of seven isn't too bad.

a better way

Give the deck a quick shuffle yourself, glimpse the bottom card and keep track of it when they are spread face-down on the table.

Call the name of that card first, and then pick it up as the last of the six or seven cards you call, and you will be 100 percent correct.

NOTE: The one-ahead system has been—and is being—widely used in various "mind-reading" effects. In its simplest version, you pass about six or seven small pads and pencils to various members of your audience, including one to a confederate. Have them write down their questions, fold their slips and drop them into your hat, which you then carry to your table.

Keep track of the location of your confederate's slip, stir up the rest, and pick any slip but his out of the hat and hold it to your forehead.

After a bit of concentration, say the question you and your confederate have prearranged: "I am beginning to get an impression . . . A person—a gentleman, I believe, wants to know whether to take a certain long trip he is contemplating in the near future [or whatever]. Let's see if that is correct . . ."

Open the slip you have held to your forehead and (to yourself) read and remember the question it contains. Out loud, pretend to read your confederate's question about the long trip, which you have previously memorized. Say, "Was that correct? Is someone here thinking about a trip?"

Your confederate confirms that he was, and then you go on to answer the question for him, but in a general, fun way.

Pick up another slip, hold it to your forehead, ask your audience to concentrate along with you, and read out the essence—not the exact words—of the last question you just read to yourself, answer it, open it, have it confirmed and continue in that fashion.

You are now a mind reader!

magic squares ★

*fascinating mathematical
oddities*

Magic squares are among the most interesting of mathematical oddities. There are many, many types and hundreds of methods for making them. Following is one of the easiest ways, and fun to do and to show.

1 Make a nine-box square and place 1 in the top center.

2 2 goes one up and one to the right, but since we have no box there, we drop it to the bottom of that column.

3 3 goes one up and one to the right, but because there is no box there, and no place to drop it, we move it as far to the left as we can.

4 4 would go one up and one to the right, but since that box is occupied by the 1, we drop the 4 underneath the 3.

5 5 goes one up and one to the right, and

6 so does the 6.

7 We have no box for the 7, so we drop it under the 6.

8 There is no box for the 8, so we bring it over to the left.

9 There is no room for the 9, so we drop it to the bottom of the next column.

Our magic square is complete. The sum of each column, including the diagonals, adds up to 15.

We could have started with any number provided we placed it in the center of the top row.

A magic square of five across, or any odd number, works the same way. Even numbered squares require a different method. If magic squares intrigue you, there is an interesting chapter on the subject in *Greater Magic* by John Northern Hilliard.

8	1	6
3	5	7
4	9	2

17	24	1	8	15
23	5	7	14	16
4	6	13	20	22
10	12	19	21	3
11	18	25	2	9

finding hidden objects ★

*a test of the magician's
powers of ESP*

the effect

The magician leaves the room, and while he is
gone someone hides a small object. He returns
and the spectators "will" him to precisely where
the object is hidden.

to prepare

You require a trusted confederate and a simple
code for this highly effective trick.

Before you begin, your confederate and you agree
on a starting point in the room (let's call it
twelve o'clock) in which you are going to do the
trick. With your back to twelve o'clock, mentally
divide the room into four quadrants.

Each quadrant can be further divided into four
smaller quadrants, and so on, which makes it
possible to zero in on almost the precise spot in
which the object is hidden.

Your confederate secretly signals the proper
quadrants with a simple hand code. As he or she
sits relaxed, hand on lap, the protruding finger
(one finger for the first quadrant, two for the
second, and so forth) signals which quadrant of
the room the object is hidden. As soon as you
are in the first quadrant, your confederate directs
you to the next, and so on, until the object
is found.

to perform

You speak briefly about the scientific validity of ESP, "brain waves" or the like and offer a practical demonstration. You leave the room, and while you are gone, a previously agreed upon object is hidden. The spectators concentrate on the object and you pick up their "brain waves" (and your confederate's secret signals). Eventually you find the object.

twelve o'clock

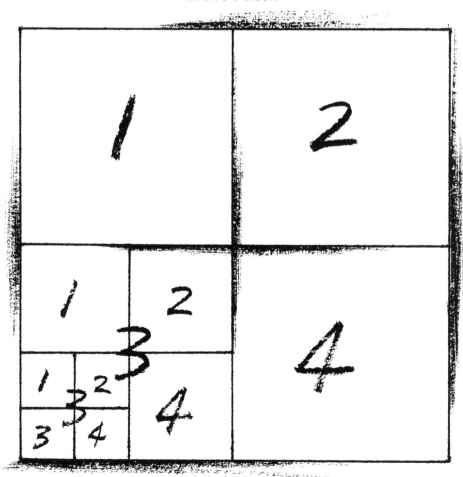

X-ray eyes ★★

the effect

The magician has several volunteers from the audience blindfold him, but despite their thoroughness he manages to call off the serial numbers of dollar bills, read the dates on coins, even drive a car through crowded city streets and perform other seemingly impossible feats.

to prepare

Despite the blindfolds, the performer does actually see. There are several ways to accomplish this.

impromptu version

Fold a handkerchief, or better yet, a colored bandanna, as illustrated. In this case, it is probably best if you put it on yourself.

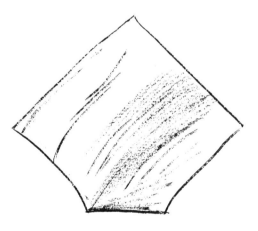

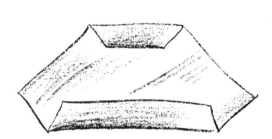

Upper and lower flaps overlap

When you put the blindfold on, spread the edges apart so that you are looking through one layer of cloth.

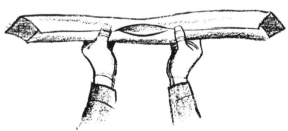

a more professional blindfold

several layers of black or navy-blue cloth so that the blindfold is absolutely opaque (approximately 3½ inches by 18 inches long)

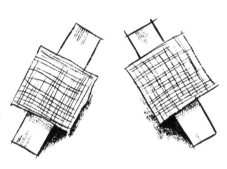

roll of 1½-inch-wide adhesive tape of a type that comes off easily and painlessly

1 ¾-inch-square pads of surgical gauze

Tear off three strips of 1½-inch tape and attach to a smooth surface so they can be easily obtained.

Have blindfold affixed as illustrated.

With this blindfold in place you should be able to sight down the sides of your nose and see enough to read serial numbers, to name objects and so on.

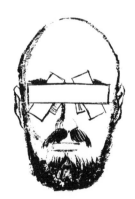

Memorize the shoes your friends or certain members of your audience are wearing beforehand, and you will be able to address those persons by name merely by glimpsing their shoes.

to perform

Blindfolds are usually just pieces of utility apparatus used during certain tricks. Some magicians, however, have built entire acts around their so-called X-ray eyes.

One famous performer called off the dates on coins, identified objects, avoided obstacles placed on stage, and walked through crowded rooms without colliding with anyone.

A few could actually total figures written on a blackboard, and even fire rifles with surprising accuracy.

Joseph Dunninger, a well-known mentalist, would have the local newspaper reporters blindfold him and then would drive a car through town. This was a great stunt used to garner publicity and thus attract audiences to his performances.

One old-time mentalist used to drive a horse-drawn buggy through town to find some small, hidden object, and he did it while heavily blindfolded!

Some performers have balls of dough placed against their eyes and under the blindfolds. Others have silver dollars taped over their eyes and under the blindfold. Sometimes a cloth or paper bag is placed right over the performer's head.

In the case of the paper bag, the performer makes a secret pinhole in front of each eye. The cloth bag, which the performer supplies, is gimmicked by having a thin spot which he maneuvers in front of his eyes.

If you are interested in this type of an act, experiment with various types of blindfolds, and as usual, practice, practice, practice.

super memory ★★★

a very astounding demonstration
of mental agility

---

the effect

The magician explains that he is going to memorize a full deck of cards. He turns his back and tosses three ping-pong balls over his shoulder into the audience to prove that his selection of helpers is pure chance, which it is.

The spectators who catch the balls come up on stage. One of them stands by a large blackboard on which the numbers 1 through 52 appear. The other two inspect a deck of cards, shuffle it thoroughly and divide it between them.

The magician stands onstage where he can't possibly see the blackboard and requests that his assistants call off the cards one at a time at intervals of about a second or so while the helper at the blackboard records them in numerical order.

When all of the cards have been called off, the magician, without so much as a glance at the blackboard, calls off the entire deck in the precise order in which the cards were recorded. Then, just as rapidly, he calls off the entire deck backwards.

When any member of the audience shouts out a number between 1 and 52, the magician names the card at that number, and conversely, when any card is called off, the magician instantly calls the number at which that card appears.

How does he do it? Very simple. He really memorizes the cards!

to prepare

Obviously you would require an incredible memory to memorize the order and position of every card in the deck. There may be a few unusually gifted persons who are capable of it, but the rest of us ordinary mortals have to rely on a system, and happily there is a system that is relatively easy to learn. It is called mnemonics or memory by association.

The essence of the system depends on associating a specific visual image with the object you are trying to commit to memory. For example, aboard ship the port light is red and the starboard light is green. It is easy enough to memorize that, but easier still if you associate port with wine (port wine) and remember that wine is red. The remaining light, starboard, is the one that is green.

That is the basic system. In order to use it, however, you have to commit to memory a master list of 52 objects in numerical sequence. Then, when any object is called out, you immediately link it with the first object on your list, which happens to be hat. The second is hen, the third is ham, and then hair, hill and so on.

When you memorize the list, however, you don't merely remember hat or hen or ham and let it go at that. Instead you try to visualize the most outstanding or the most ludicrous or in some way the most memorable object you can. For example, instead of a conventional hat, you might envision a tall plug hat with a crown that's flopping in the breeze. Instead of an ordinary hen, you might envision an enormously fat hen or an extraordinarily thin one or possibly a very mean hen who is constantly pecking at everything in sight. In other words, you create an image that is so indelible you couldn't forget it even if you tried.

To make it easier for you, there is a list of sounds which are associated with the numbers from one to ten. Once you have thoroughly learned the sounds and the numbers with which they go, you'll find it easier to memorize the master list. Note, for example, that the third sound is M. Number 3 on the master list is haM, 13 is teaM, 23 is gnoMe, 33 is MuMMy, and 43 is raM. Note also that all the objects in the third sequence of ten—the thirties—start with M. So far as possible, the master list adheres to this system. Unfortunately there are some exceptions because the amount of objects which start with a particular letter are limited, but in any event learn the following list of sounds. It will make memorizing the master list, and the card list, much easier.

1. T	6. SH	
2. N	7. C, G	
3. M	8. V	
4. R	9. P, B	
5. L	10. D, S	

When you are thoroughly conversant with the
list of sounds, you are ready to proceed with the
master list.

1. haT	19. TuB	37. MuG
2. heN	20. NoSe	38. MuFF
3. haM	21. winDoW	39. MoP
4. haiR	22. NuN	40. RoSe
5. hiLL	23. gNoMe	41. RaT
6. SHoe	24. NeRo	42. RaiN
7. Cow	25. NaiL	43. RaM
8. hiVe	26. NiCHe	44. RoweR
9. aPe	27. NaG	45. RaiL
10. wooDS	28. NiFe	46. RaSH
11. TiDe	29. NoB	47. RaCk
12. TiN	30. MouSe	48. Raft
13. TeaM	31. MaT	49. Rug
14. TiRe	32. MaN	50. LaSS
15. TeLevision	33. MuMMy	51. LaNyard
16. diSH	34. MayoR	52. LiNe
17. doG	35. MiLL	
18. doVe	36. MaT	

After you have committed this list to memory
you are ready to memorize any 52 objects called
out by your audience. To give you a practical idea
of how it works, let's assume that the following
objects are called off to you.

bird
pencil
tree
elephant
and so forth

The instant you hear "bird," you might envision
a live bird trying desperately to escape from the
interior of the old plug hat you know is number
one, or any other image you can dream up in a
hurry.

For "pencil" you might envision a long, yellow
pencil sticking out of the chicken that represents number two.

For "tree" a good image might be a tree full of fat, greasy, dripping hams.

"Elephant" should make a good image with any number. You might envision an elephant with long, golden hair, and so on right down the line. Then when someone calls out "three," you automatically think of ham and immediately recall hams in a tree. You'll be amazed and delighted at how easy it is and how well you do it when you have learned the master list thoroughly.

In order to memorize a deck of cards you have to give each card a specific image, and that means memorizing an additional list 52 long. This list utilizes the same sequence of sounds. I think you will find it easier to memorize than the first.

Note that all the objects in each suit begin with a like letter—H for hearts, D for diamonds, S for spades and C for clubs. The aces are what they are, and an attempt has been made to rhyme the picture cards with the object that represents it.

1 H	Heart	1 D	Diamond	1 C	Club	1 S	Spade
2 H	HoNk	2 D	DeN	2 C	CaN	2 S	SuN
3 H	HeM	3 D	DaM	3 C	CaMp	3 S	SuM
4 H	HaRe	4 D	DooR	4 C	CoRe	4 S	SoRe
5 H	HaiL	5 D	DoLL	5 C	CeLL	5 S	SaiL
6 H	HaSH	6 D	DaSH	6 C	CaSH	6 S	SaSH
7 H	HoG	7 D	DoCk	7 C	CoCK	7 S	SoCK
8 H	HooF	8 D	DiVe	8 C	Cave	8 S	SaFe
9 H	HuB	9 D	DeB	9 C	CaP	9 S	SaP
10 H	HoSe	10 D	DoSe	10 C	CaSe	10 S	SuDs
Jack H	Hack	Jack D	Drag	Jack C	Crack	Jack S	Sack
Queen H	Queen	Queen D	Dream	Queen C	Cream	Queen S	Steam
King H	Hinge	King D	Drink	King C	King	King S	Sing

Let us assume that the following cards are called out.

9C   6H   10H

You do essentially what you did when you memorized a list of objects, but in this case you associate the two images you have memorized.

For example, for 9C you envision your plug hat (number 1) wearing a cap (9C).

For the 6H you might envision your skinny hen (number 2) struggling to escape from a pile of corn beef hash (6H).

For 10H envision a powerful jet of water from a hose buffeting your greasy ham (number 3) about.

Once you have memorized both lists you are ready—at least theoretically—to display your prowess to the world. The procedure outlined above under "the effect" is a good one to follow, but please bear this in mind: unless you can really memorize a full deck of cards rapidly, unhesitatingly and well, you run a grave risk of putting your audience to sleep. You probably would do best by starting with half a deck. If that goes well and your audience seems to be genuinely entertained, then increase the amount of cards at your next show and see how it goes.

I have seen an old-timer memorize two entire decks of cards and do it superbly well, too. He could memorize cards almost as quickly as they were called off to him, and he could call them back even faster, but despite the fact that he was an absolute master and gave an amazing exhibition, it did get a bit boring after a while.

That, basically, is the mnemonics system, tried and true and used for many, many years. If the subject interests you, Harry Lorayne, who is a great card man and perhaps this nation's leading memory expert, has with Jerry Lucas written a superb volume called *The Memory Book* that can make you an expert.

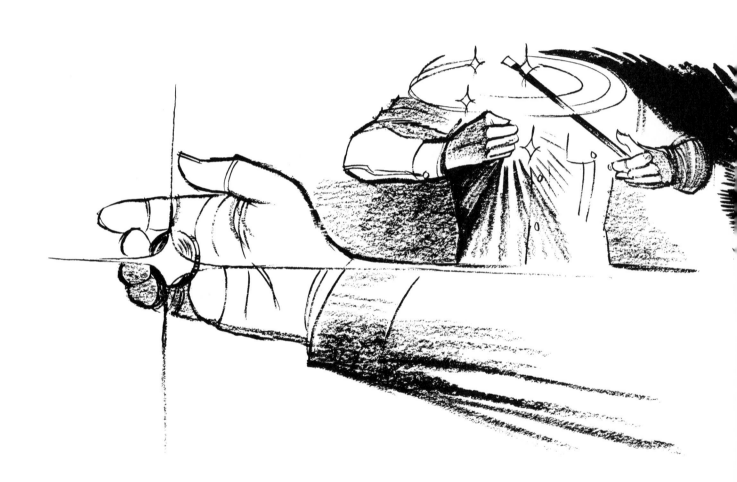

close-up
magic

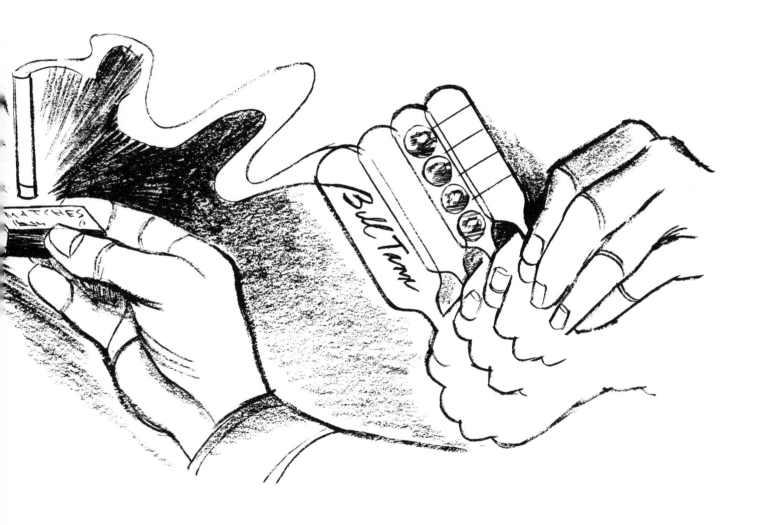

vanishing small objects

several highly deceptive
non-sleight-of-hand methods

paper-fold vanish ★ ★

This is a very deceptive vanish, and while it doesn't require sleight of hand in the true sense of the word, like everything else in magic, it does require a certain amount of practice.

Fold the paper over the coin.

Fold the left third of the paper in front.

Fold the right third of the paper in front.

Fold the top portion in front.

Casually press the paper firmly over the coin to make a visible impression of the coin.

As you handle the paper, turn it upside-down, allowing the coin to fall into your right hand, where you grip it in your fingers (see finger palm, page 22). The instant this happens, carry the paper up and away with your left as you say, "Keep your eyes on the coin . . ." and reach for your wand. Drop the coin on your table or into the servante as you pick up the wand.

Wave the wand over the paper.

Place the wand down, and tear the paper into pieces.

The coin has vanished!

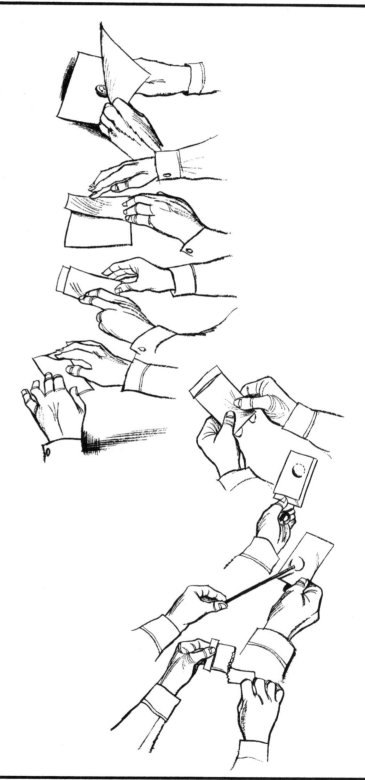

handkerchief vanish ★

The magician shows a coin at the fingertips of his left hand. He throws a handkerchief over the coin and invites several people to reach under and feel the coin to make sure it is still there.

He whips the handkerchief away, and the coin is gone!

how it is done

The last person to reach under the handkerchief was your confederate. He merely removed the coin and kept it hidden in his hand.

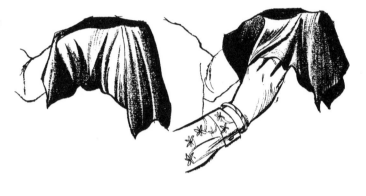

the coin pull ★

There are few vanishes that are as clean as those performed with a pull, and they take relatively little skill to do well. Getting the pull into your hand ready to use is the biggest problem.

Pin the pull under your jacket or up your sleeve. It works well from either place, but is more difficult to obtain from your sleeve.

This move takes practice too. Don't ever show it—or anything—until you have practiced it to perfection in front of your mirror!

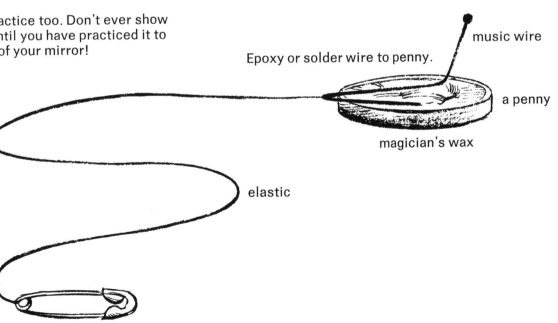

Epoxy or solder wire to penny.

music wire

a penny

magician's wax

elastic

silk pull ★

still the easiest and cleanest vanish of a silk

The magician tucks a silk into his left hand. He snaps his fingers, the silk vanishes, and both hands are shown unmistakably empty.

small plastic medicine vial

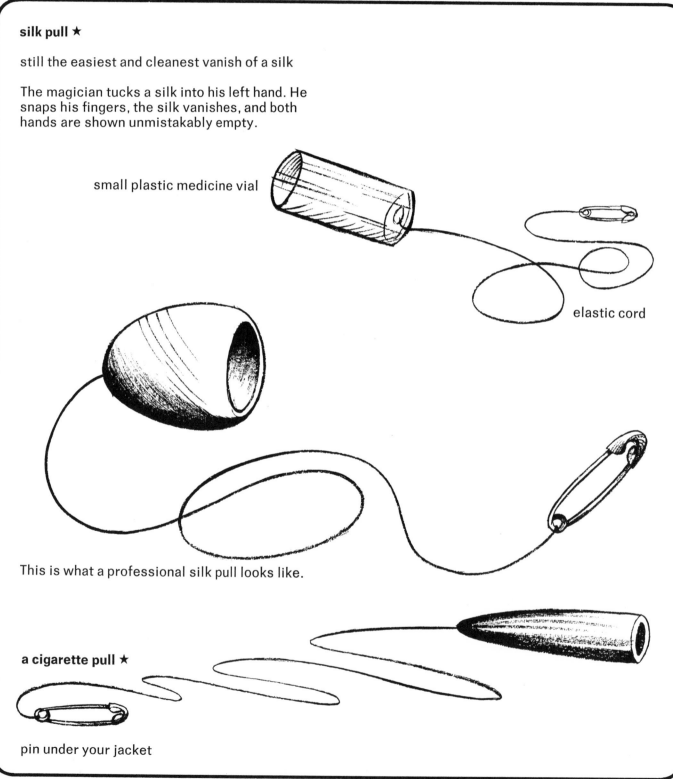

elastic cord

This is what a professional silk pull looks like.

a cigarette pull ★

pin under your jacket

the rising cigarette ★

*despite its simplicity,
a really effective little trick*

the effect

The magician displays a matchbox. He sets a cigarette—lit or unlit—on the box, where it stands unaided and then slowly rises two inches or so above the box.

to prepare

Bend a fine wire (music wire is best) as illustrated and paint it dead black.

Prop the wire up on your table so that you can easily slip your left pinky into it without fumbling. (A speck of wax will do the trick.)

Place an ordinary matchbox and a cigarette on your table in front of the wire.

to perform

Pick up the matchbox with your left hand, and at the same time, slip your left pinky into the wire.

Hold the box and the wire as illustrated.

Pick up the cigarette with your right hand and set it on the wire.

Make the cigarette rise by raising your left pinky.

NOTE: You can use a burning wooden match instead of a cigarette, but first bore a fine hole in the base for the wire.

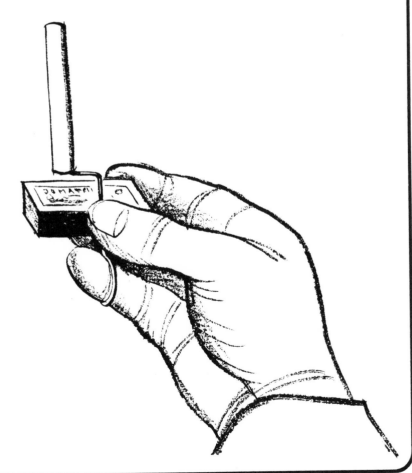

ring on string ★★

takes some practice but
it's worth the effort

the effect

The magician has his audience examine a small metal ring and a length of string. A spectator is asked to thread the ring on the string and hold both ends securely. The magician throws a handkerchief over the string, reaches under and removes the ring.

to prepare

Place a handkerchief and a metal ring about an inch and a half in diameter in your right trouser or jacket pocket. Place a duplicate ring and a piece of soft string around two and a half feet long in your left jacket or trouser pocket.

to perform

1 Remove the ring and the string from your pocket and ask a spectator to examine both.

2 Have the spectator thread the ring on the string and hold both ends tightly.

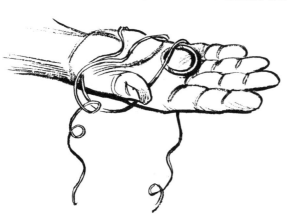

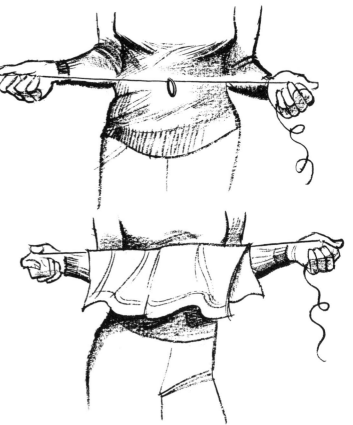

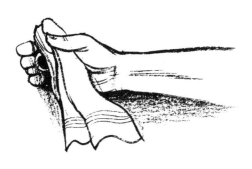

3 Reach into your right-hand pocket, immediately finger-palm the duplicate ring, and bring out the handkerchief.

4 Cover the ring with the handkerchief. Reach under the handkerchief with both hands, cover the ring with your left hand and slide it to your left.

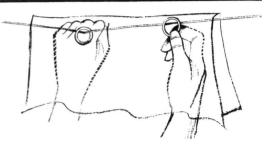

5 With your right hand, place the duplicate ring against the string and ask for a bit of slack.

6 Hold the ring with the thumb and first finger of the left hand, and with the fingers of the right hand pull the slackened string through the ring and over the top as illustrated.

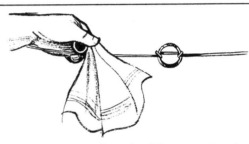

7 Remove the handkerchief by grasping it at the top center between the thumb and first and second fingers of the right hand and transfer it to the left hand, where it is held by the left thumb and first finger, which are still concealing the original ring.

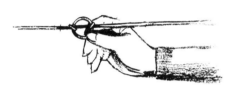

8 Hold the duplicate ring at your fingertips to prevent it from slipping off the string and say to the spectator,

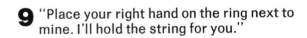

9 "Place your right hand on the ring next to mine. I'll hold the string for you."

10 Slide your left hand (and the ring) over and grasp the string, thus freeing his right hand.

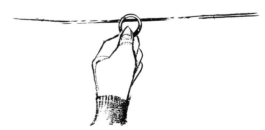

11 When he grasps the attached ring, release your hold on it and allow him to remove it.

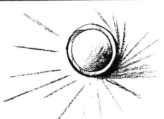

12 As he does, release your hold on the string, step back and drop the palmed ring into your pocket.

the phantom cigarette ★★

old but good magic

the effect

The magician rolls an imaginary cigarette and carefully places it between his lips. He takes his matchbox, strikes a match, and suddenly, magically, is puffing away at a real cigarette.

to prepare

Cut an opening in a matchbox, place a cigarette in it as illustrated, and place it on your table or in your pocket.

to perform

Tell your audience that you have been lucky enough to have obtained a supply of the world's first invisible tobacco, and then very realistically demonstrate the art of cigarette rolling with your imaginary props. When your cigarette is finished, place it between your lips and reach into your pocket or onto your table for your matchbox.

Hold the box in your left hand, remove a match and close the box. With your hands cupped in front of your mouth, as though to shield your light from the wind, strike the match, and as the box comes close to your mouth, grasp the end of the cigarette in your lips, bring your hands forward a trifle and in the same motion light the cigarette.

Take a deep puff as you place the matchbox into your pocket.

This is an old trick that has stood the test of time; it is very effective when it is well presented, so practice hard.

string and straw trick ★

Joseph Kolar's very mystifying cut and restored string

the effect

The magician openly threads a string through an ordinary drinking straw. He hands a pair of scissors to a spectator and has him snip the top of the straw off, but the string is instantly restored.

to prepare

Use a razor blade to cut a two-inch-long slit in the center of an ordinary drinking straw.

to perform

Have a number of drinking straws in a glass on your table. Casually select the gimmicked straw and thread a length of string through it. (A wide straw and a fairly stiff piece of string make this much easier.)

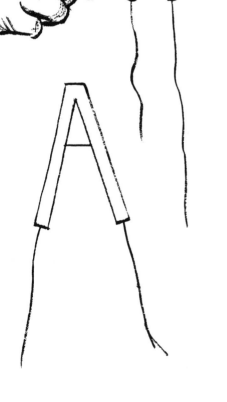

Bend the straw in half.

Hold the straw as illustrated, and as you even the ends, pull the string through the slit.

Concealing the string with your thumb, have the spectator cut through the top of the straw.

Push the ends of the straw together, remove the string and show it restored.

paddle trick ★

*entertaining, easy to do,
and really deceptive*

the effect

The magician shows a small wooden paddle on both sides. A drawing of a small fish is seen at the base. The magician rubs his finger over the drawing and the fish swims to the top of the paddle.

to prepare

Cut a paddle, shaped as illustrated, from a doctor's tongue depressor or any thin strip of wood. Draw a small fish at the base of the paddle on one side and draw the same fish at the top of the paddle on the other side.

to perform

The paddle trick requires sleight of hand, but the move is very simple and easily learned.

Practice the following moves until you can do them smoothly.

1 Push your thumb over to the left, twisting the paddle over.

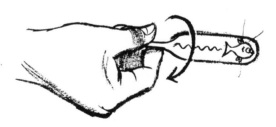

2 Pull your thumb back in the opposite direction.

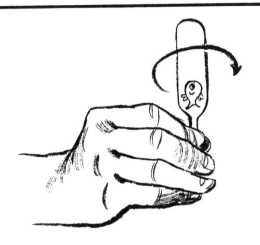

3 Repeat the twist, but this time

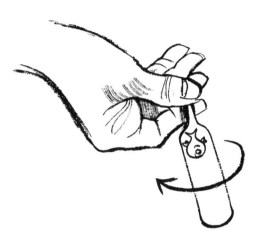

4 pivot the hand at the wrist as you do so.

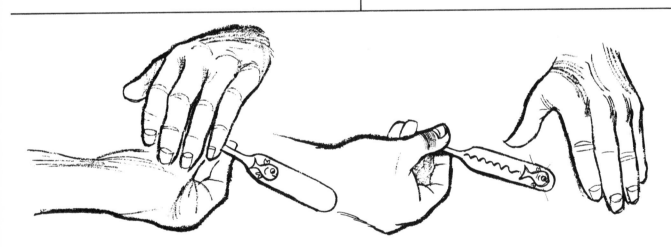

In reality you are only showing one side of the paddle.

When you can do the moves smoothly and well, you are ready to do the trick.

Show the paddle, apparently on both sides, so that the fish appears to be at the base of both sides.

Pass your left hand over the paddle as you twist it to the other side, but don't pivot your hand as you do so.

The fish appears to have swum to the top.

Show that the fish is now at the top of both sides of the paddle.

paddle variation #1 ★

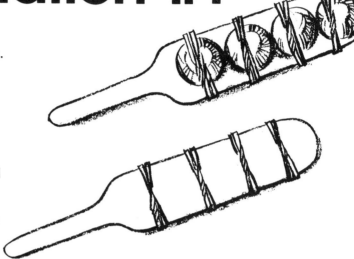

to prepare

Make a second paddle, but leave this one blank.

Secure four pennies to one side of the paddle with four small rubber bands.

to perform

Show that the paddle contains nothing but four rubber bands by using the previously explained move.

Run your hand across the surface of the paddle and under its cover, and twist the pennies into view!

paddle variation #2 ★

to prepare

Across the face of the paddle, write the name of a person to whom you know you will be showing the trick.

Cover the paddle with pennies as in Variation #1.

to perform

Show nothing but four rubber bands on either side of the paddle.

Materialize the pennies.

Hold the paddle pennies-side-down over the spectator's hand.

Remove the rubber bands, allowing the pennies to fall into his hand.

Show that both sides of the paddle are blank.

Materialize the spectator's name.

144

the great matchbox escape ★

a cute little trick that's fun to do

the effect

The magician threads a matchbox on a piece of tape or ribbon, the ends of which are held by two spectators. He throws a handkerchief over the box, reaches under and removes the box while the tapes are still firmly held.

to prepare

Cut apart a matchbox and carefully stick it back together with two dabs of magician's wax or any soft, sticky wax available.

to perform

Show the matchbox and openly thread a length of tape or ribbon through it.

Ask two spectators to hold the tape at either end.

Show a large, empty handkerchief and throw it over the matchbox.

Standing behind the box so as not to block the audience's view, reach under the handkerchief, unfasten the box, slip it off the tape, quickly stick it back together again, and bring it out from under the handkerchief.

The matchbox has apparently penetrated the tape!

squash ★

*the perfect vanish of a
small glass of liquid*

the effect

The magician displays a shot glass filled with
liquid. He squeezes the glass between his hands,
and glass and contents vanish!

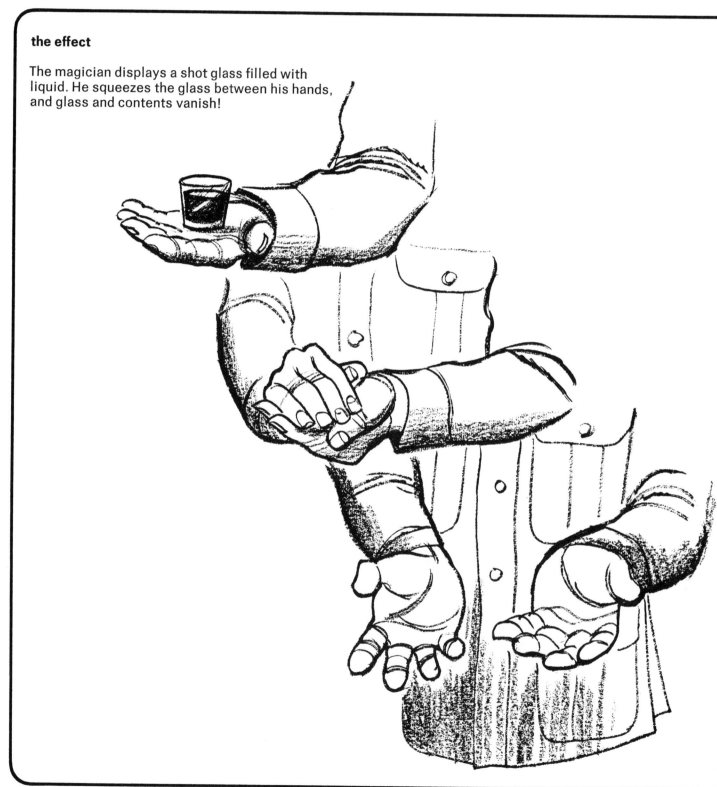

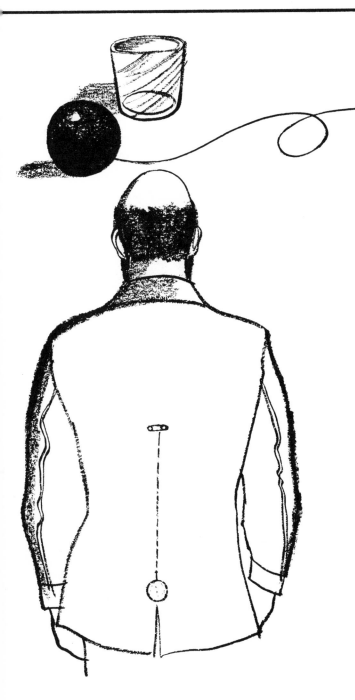

to prepare

Obtain a standard small shot glass and a solid rubber ball the diameter of which is slightly larger than that of the glass.

Drive a hole through the ball with a nail or an ice pick and thread a fairly heavy, round elastic cord about fourteen inches long through it.

Tie a small button on one end and a heavy safety pin on the other.

Pin the device (it is called a "pull") to the inside of your jacket at the back so that the ball hangs about four inches above the bottom of your jacket.

to perform

Pick up the shot glass of liquid with your right hand and transfer it to your left palm.

As you display the glass, turn slightly to your right, and while attention is directed to the glass, "steal" the ball with your right hand.

Lower your left to about waist level, bring the right hand (and the ball) over the left, and force the ball into the glass.

The instant the ball is securely lodged in the glass, release the pressure on the ball, which will snap back under your jacket carrying the glass of liquid with it.

Separate your hands and show them empty.

NOTE: Experiment in front of your mirror. Work out your presentation and misdirection so that you can steal the pull and effect the vanish smoothly and undetectably, and you'll have a stunning effect to add to your repertoire.

miscellaneous magic

ring on the rope mystery ★★

simple and easy to do,
but a real puzzler

the effect

The magician exhibits a length of rope (about four feet) and a solid wooden ring. He has a spectator examine the ring while another ties one end of the rope to each of the magician's wrists. The magician holds the ring at his fingertips while a large scarf is draped over his hands. When the scarf is pulled away a few moments later, the ring is seen dangling on the rope, which is still secured to his wrists.

to prepare

Slip a duplicate ring up on your forearm where it is hidden by your jacket.

to perform

Pass the ring and the rope out for examination.

Have your wrists tied as illustrated.

Take the ring back and hold it at your fingertips.

Ask someone to throw the scarf over your hands.

Under its cover, immediately place the ring in your inside jacket pocket and pull the duplicate ring down your arm, over your wrist and onto the rope.

Have the scarf pulled off your hands, or toss it off yourself, and exhibit the ring on the rope.

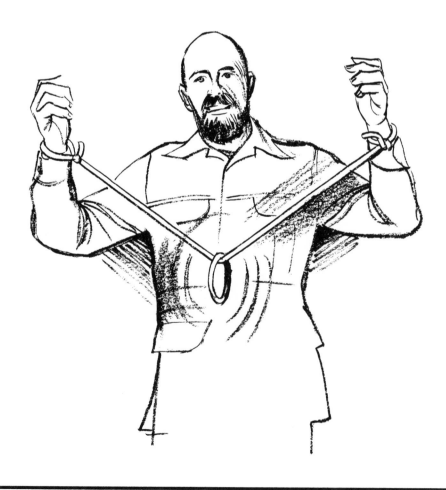

150

the paper tree ★

*not magic, but a pretty
effect anyway*

the effect

The magician displays a roll of
paper. He holds the tube in his
left hand, inserts his forefinger
into the center, and pulls the
inside of the tube out to form a
tree.

to prepare

Roll a tabloid-sized sheet of
newspaper into a tube, glue a
second sheet onto the first, and
repeat until you have rolled up
three or four sheets.

Colorful wrapping paper will
produce a prettier tree.

to perform

Pick up the tube and tear or use
a heavy pair of scissors to cut
the tube as illustrated. Then
simply pull up the center.

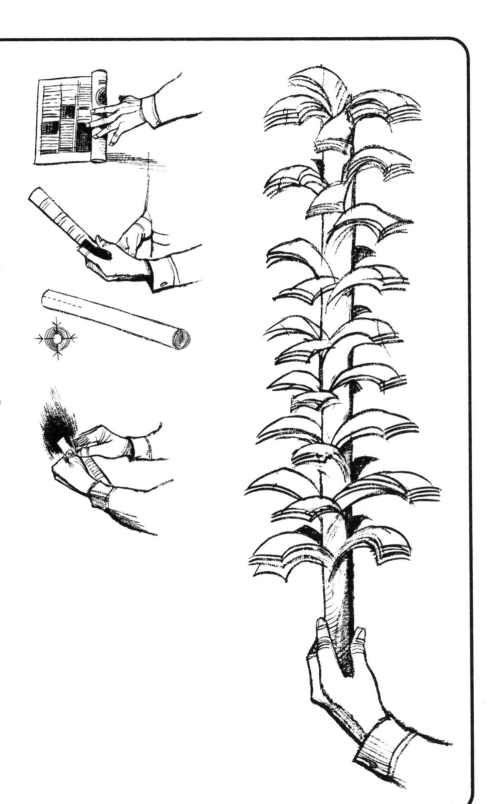

comedy flower growth ★

*a funny running gag,
tried and tested*

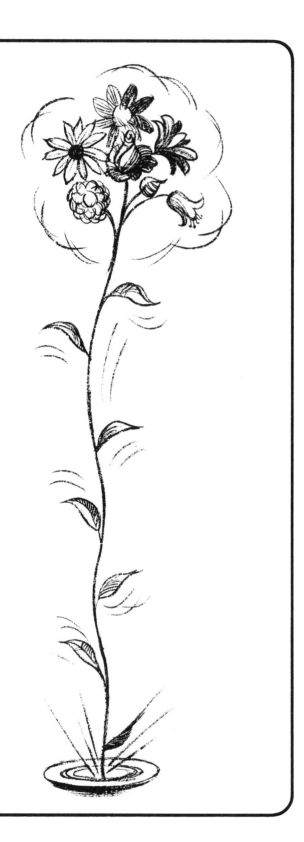

the effect

The magician pours some water into a bowl sitting on his table and a bunch of flowers suddenly pops into view. At intervals he pours more water into the bowl, and every time he does, the plant visibly grows several feet taller.

to prepare

Sew a bouquet of artificial flowers onto a fifteen-foot length of soft cotton rope dyed green. If you like, sew an occasional leaf on the rope at intervals of a foot or two.

Set the rope-stem into a wide-mouthed bowl and drop the flowers in on top.

Attach a strong black thread to the flowers and run it straight up to a pulley hidden in the flies, and across and down into the wings where it can be secretly pulled by your assistant.

to perform

Pick up your watering can and pour some water into the bowl. As you do so, have your offstage assistant pull the plant up a couple of feet.

At various intervals during your show water the plant until, by evening's end, it has grown almost up to the ceiling.

the cornucopia vanish ★

an easily made device for
vanishing a silk

the effect

The magician shows a small square of newspaper. He rolls it into a cone and pokes a silk into it. He waves his hand over the cone and opens it up to show that the silk has vanished.

to prepare

Cut a piece of newspaper, fold on the dotted line, and glue with rubber cement at points BC.

Form a cone as illustrated.

Show a small silk and with your wand or a pen poke it into pocket.

Wave your hand over the cone, and open it to show that the silk has vanished.

Casually crumple up the cone and toss it away.

NOTE: Make the cone as large—or small—as required to indetectably vanish the item you are working with.

This cone may also be used to vanish torn cards and other nonbulky objects.

the magic mouse ★

an old favorite of street pitchmen
and still as amusing as ever

the effect

The magician places a small wax mouse on his palm. At his urging the mouse scurries across his hands, up his arms and so forth.

to prepare

Fashion a small mouse out of wax. Softened candle wax will do, but beeswax or dental wax is better.

Obtain a dark (black is best) hair about fifteen inches long. Tie several knots in each end, and affix two small pellets of magician's wax.

Stick one pellet to the underside of the mouse and the other to your middle shirt or jacket button.

Put the mouse in a matchbox, and with the hair in place, slip the box into your jacket pocket.

to perform

Tell the audience about your pet mouse.

Remove the box from your pocket, open it very carefully, take out the mouse and place it on your left palm.

Slowly move your hand away from your body, alternating hands, and your mouse scurries about as though alive.

Actually he doesn't really move, but the motion of your hands creates a perfect illusion.

Experiment in front of your mirror. Coax him, pet him, urge him on. The better an actor you are, the better the illusion you create.

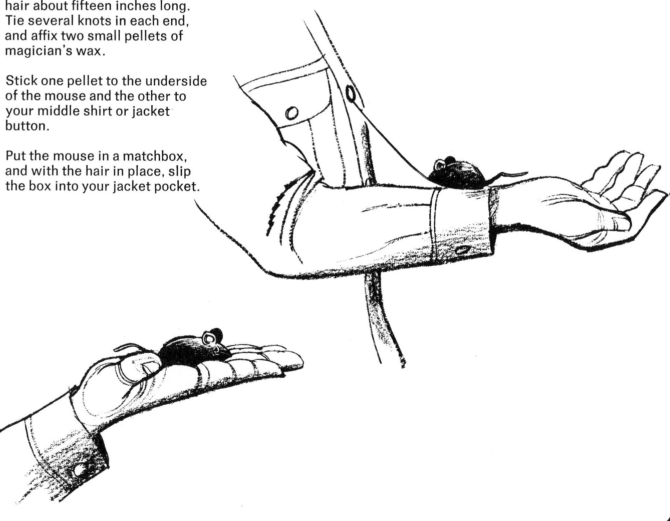

snip-snip ★

*the easiest trick in the world,
but mystifying nevertheless*

the effect

The magician exhibits a strip of
newspaper about an inch wide
and fourteen inches long. He
folds the strip in half, and
distinctly cuts it in two. When
he opens the strip, it is restored.

to prepare

Cut a sheet of newspaper into strips about an
inch wide and about fourteen inches or so long.

Brush the center area with ordinary rubber
cement and allow it to dry.

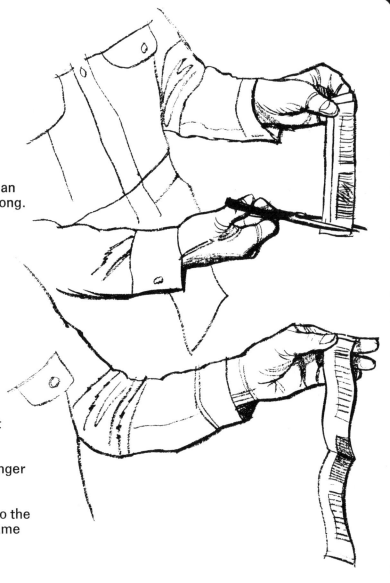

to perform

Show a strip of paper, fold it in half, and cut
across the folded end as illustrated.

Hold one end between the thumb and forefinger
of the left hand, and let the other fall.

The strip is automatically restored thanks to the
secret application of rubber cement. The same
strip may be cut again and again.

wand from purse ★

*the magical production of
a wand*

the effect

The magician displays a small change purse. He opens it up, reaches in and pulls out a full-sized wand.

to prepare

Obtain a small change purse, and cut a slit a little over an inch long in the bottom.

Place your wand up your left sleeve, or if it is too long, fasten it under your jacket as illustrated.

to perform

Reach into your pocket for your change purse, open it up, extract a couple of coins if you like, and then reach in and slowly pull out your wand.

Close your purse, put it away, rap your wand to prove it's solid and proceed with your act.

This is a good follow-up to the vanishing wand, but of course be sure both wands are identical.

the vanishing wand ⋆

*a quick trick and a good
one too*

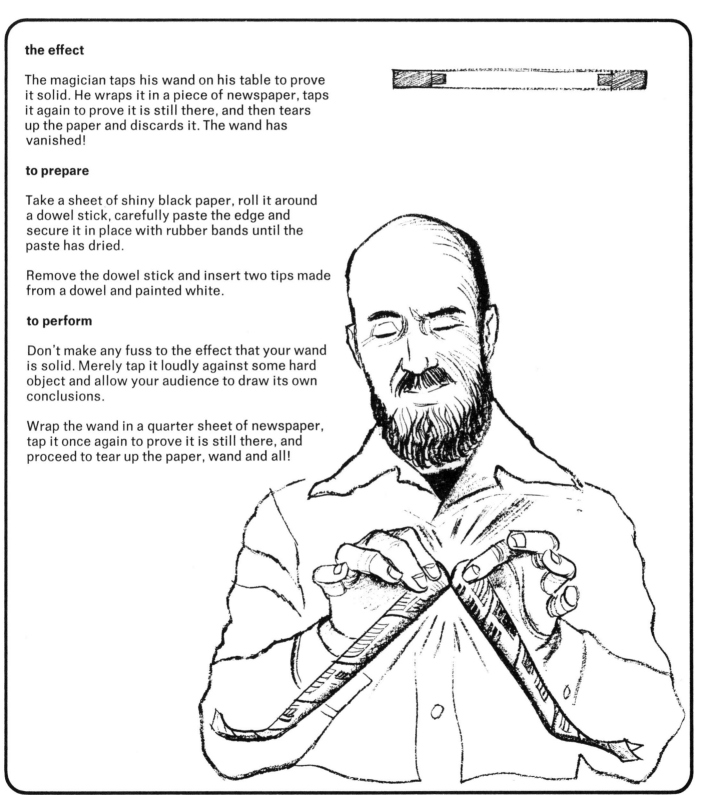

the effect

The magician taps his wand on his table to prove it solid. He wraps it in a piece of newspaper, taps it again to prove it is still there, and then tears up the paper and discards it. The wand has vanished!

to prepare

Take a sheet of shiny black paper, roll it around a dowel stick, carefully paste the edge and secure it in place with rubber bands until the paste has dried.

Remove the dowel stick and insert two tips made from a dowel and painted white.

to perform

Don't make any fuss to the effect that your wand is solid. Merely tap it loudly against some hard object and allow your audience to draw its own conclusions.

Wrap the wand in a quarter sheet of newspaper, tap it once again to prove it is still there, and proceed to tear up the paper, wand and all!

production tubes ★★

a neat way to produce
silks from an empty container

the effect

The magician shows two empty cylinders about eight inches tall and about four inches in diameter. He nests one within the other and produces a number of silks from them.

to prepare

Obtain or make two cardboard or metal cylinders, one of which is a trifle smaller in diameter than the other. A Diamond Crystal salt container is the same height as a Quaker corn meal container and just one-quarter of an inch smaller in diameter—perfect for production tubes.

Paint or cover your containers with Contact paper.

Fashion a music-wire S-hook as illustrated.

Fold six or seven fifteen-inch silks together, wrap with weak black cotton thread and hang on the hook, which hangs inside the smaller of the two cylinders.

Place both cylinders on your table.

to perform

1 Pick up the larger cylinder with your right hand and show it empty.

2 Pick up the second cylinder with your left hand and drop it into the first from the top

3 and out from the bottom. (The load will hook onto the larger cylinder.)

4 Show the second cylinder empty.

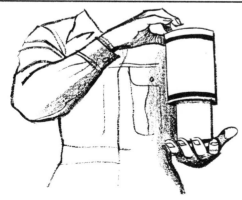

5 Set the second cylinder on your outstretched left hand and drop the first over it.

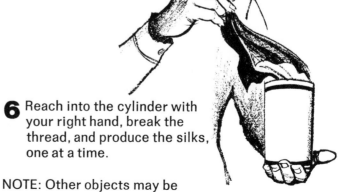

6 Reach into the cylinder with your right hand, break the thread, and produce the silks, one at a time.

NOTE: Other objects may be produced instead of silks.

instant silk ★★

*a really magical
production of a silk*

the effect

The magician shows his hands
back and front. They are
unmistakably empty. He quickly
separates his hands and a silk
appears between them
instantaneously!

to prepare

Sew a length of strong, fine
black silk thread to two adjacent
corners of a fifteen-inch silk.

Fold the silk as illustrated and
place it under your jacket with
the thread across your lapels.
(A bit of beeswax on the thread
will keep it stiff and in place.)

to perform

Hold your hands at chest height
a few inches away from your
body, palms towards the
audience.

Pivot your hands at the wrist so
that the backs face the audience.

Pivot your hands back, bringing
them a bit closer to your chest,
hook your thumbs under the
thread as you do so, and shoot
your hands out and somewhat
to each side.

The silk will open up and shoot
into your hands instantly!

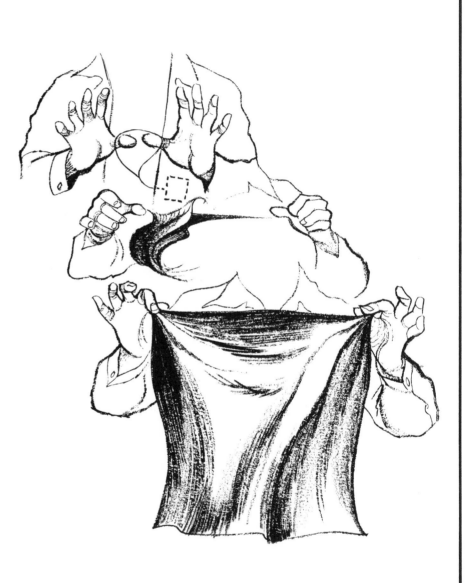

super instant silk ★★

*one of the most beautiful
silk productions ever*

to prepare

Fill a small glass with confetti of the same color as the silk you are going to produce and set on your table.

to perform

Show your hands empty as in instant silk, pick up the glass of confetti at your fingertips so your audience can plainly see that your hands are otherwise empty, and pour a mound of it onto your left hand.

Place the glass back on your table, toss the confetti into the air in the area in which the silk will emerge.

Immediately turn your hands down and inwards, hook your thumbs into the thread, and produce the silk right in the midst of the confetti shower.

the rising pencil ★

*another neat, deceptive
old-time favorite*

the effect

The magician drops a pencil into an empty wine bottle. At his command the pencil slowly rises and falls, mysteriously answering questions as it does so.

to prepare

Obtain a long, sharpened pencil without an eraser, and a tall, smoothly contoured wine bottle.

Tie several knots on each end of a length of fine black silk thread about two and a half feet long. (The actual length will depend on how and where you are showing the trick.)

Work a pellet of magician's wax about the size of a split pea onto each end of the thread.

Affix one end of the thread onto your middle jacket button and the other onto the top button.

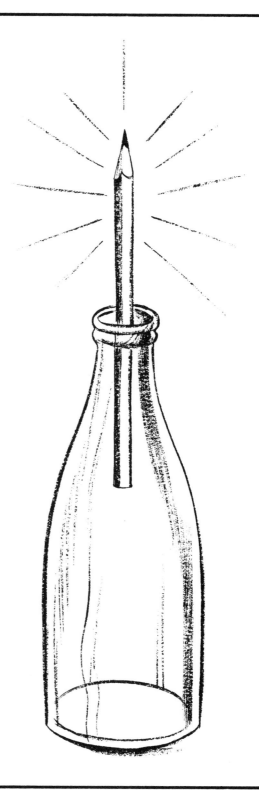

to perform

Show the pencil in the left hand and the bottle in the right.

Pass the pencil to a spectator for examination.

Pass the bottle for examination, and as you do so, secretly pick up the top pellet of wax on the fingernail of the third finger of your left hand.

Take the pencil back with your right hand and pass it to your left pressing the bottom of the pencil onto the wax pellet on your fingernail.

Take back the bottle in your right hand.

Drop the pencil, pellet end down, into the bottle and step back to your table.

Set the bottle down and control the rising and the falling of the pencil by leaning backwards and forwards, or if you prefer, hold the bottle at the bottom and make the pencil rise from that position.

NOTE: The rising pencil answers questions spectators may have. One rise means yes, two means no.

gloves to bouquet ★★

a spectacular opening effect

the effect

The magician enters, removes his gloves and tosses them into the air, where they turn into a bouquet of flowers.

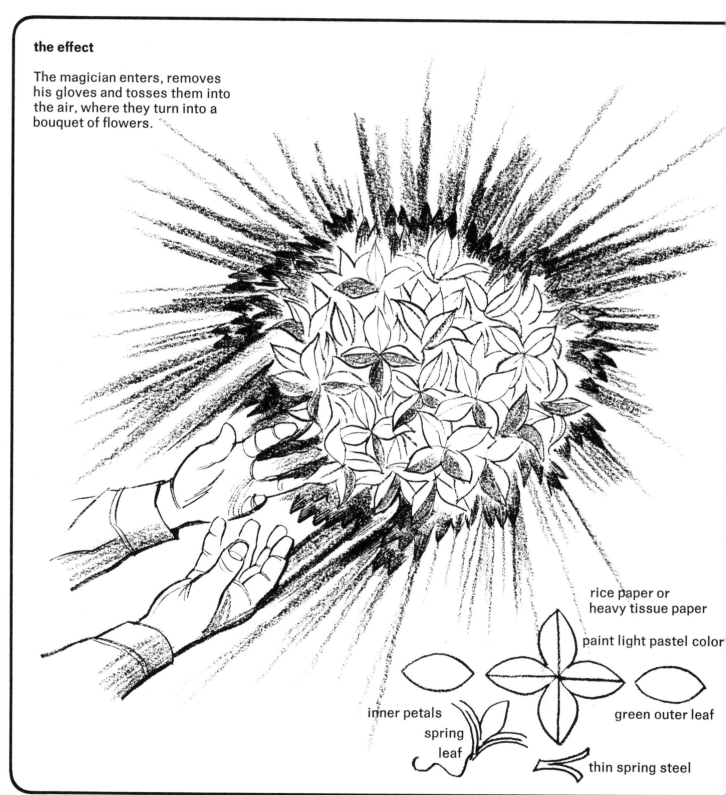

rice paper or
heavy tissue paper

paint light pastel color

inner petals

green outer leaf

spring
leaf

thin spring steel

to prepare

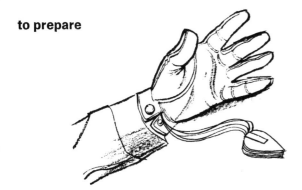

Sew or pin the strings from a bouquet of spring-flowers to the bottom of your left glove.

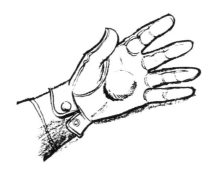

Place the folded spring-flowers in your left palm, under your glove.

to perform

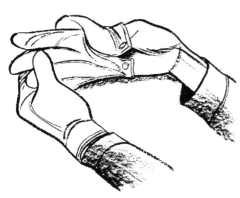

1 Remove your right glove, place it in your left hand and show your right hand empty.

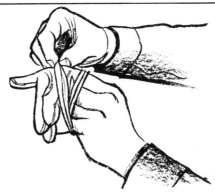

2 Remove your left glove by turning it inside out over the right glove, compress them both into a small bunch, and keep the flowers from springing open with your left thumb.

3 Toss the bunched gloves up into the air. The flowers will spring open, hiding the gloves in their midst.

4 Catch the bouquet as it comes down, and bow to your appreciative audience.

vanishing gloves ★★

a good opening trick

the effect

The magician enters wearing gloves. He ceremoniously removes his right glove and shows his hand empty. Then he removes his left glove, bunches the two together, and appears to throw them in the air, where they vanish!

to prepare

Obtain a pair of white cotton gloves (actually any thin pair will do) and sew one end of a length of heavy round black elastic to the bottom of the left glove, attach a safety pin to the other end, and affix the pin inside your jacket at the shoulder.

to perform

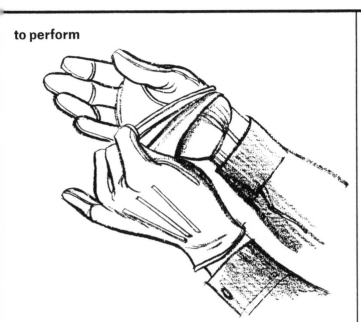

1 Remove the right glove.

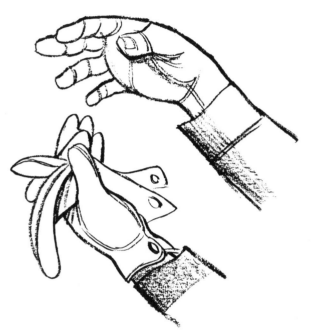

2 Holding the right glove in your left hand,

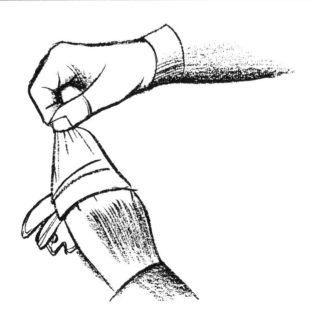

3 turn the left glove inside out over the right, and

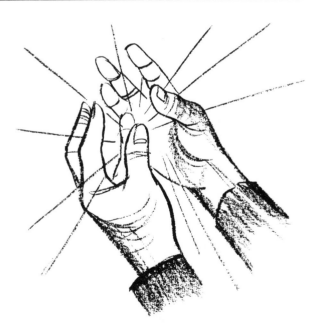

4 make a throwing motion, allowing both gloves to shoot up your left sleeve.

flowers from nowhere ★★

feather flowers are
traditional production items

the effect

The magician enters, and suddenly a large bouquet of flowers appears in each of his apparently empty hands.

to prepare

The bouquets, called feather flowers, are made of bright, colorful, highly compressible feathers. They are sold at magic shops, but you can make them yourself with less effort than you would imagine. Unless you live in a big city, your biggest problem will probably be finding the feathers.

You will need dark green feathers for leaves, and bright colors—yellows, reds, pinks, white—for the blossoms.

The stems can be round spring steel about $\frac{1}{16}$ inch or slightly less in diameter, or better yet, pieces cut from a plumber's "snake" (flat spring steel wire). Each stem should be between ten and thirteen inches long.

Rub the stem with sandpaper to clean and roughen the surface.

Bind the feathers on with strong green silk thread, and coat the bottom with glue (silicone glue is good).

Bend a one-inch ring in bottom of main center stem.

Hold the bottom of a feather bouquet in each hand, and put on your jacket. The ring should come to the base of each hand so that it can be reached by the index finger of that hand.

to perform

This trick must be done as an opener. Stride to center stage, grasp the rings with your index fingers and smartly pull both bouquets out of your sleeves.

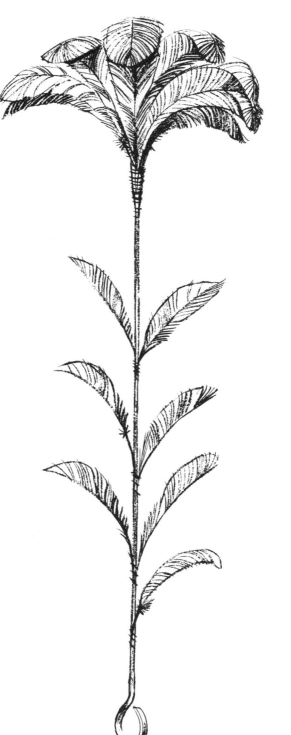

169

silk through glass ★★

*a quick, easy, different
silk trick*

the effect

The magician crumples a red silk into the bottom
of an ordinary drinking glass. He places a yellow
silk on top of it and covers all with a medium-
sized white handkerchief secured with a rubber
band. He then removes the yellow silk by pulling
it through the bottom of the solid glass!

to prepare

Obtain a red silk and a yellow one, each about
fifteen inches square, a small white handkerchief
which you place in your pocket, a rubber band
and a clear glass tumbler.

Sew a six-inch length of heavy black thread to one
corner of the yellow silk and attach a tiny black
button or tie a large knot in the other end of the
thread.

Place the handkerchief in your pocket and the
other props on your table.

to perform

Show the tumbler, tap it on the sides and bottom with your wand, and tuck the yellow silk in it so that about three inches of the black thread hangs over the side.

Crumple the red silk and place it on top of the yellow.

Remove your white handkerchief, open it, and spread it over the top of the glass and secure it with a rubber band near the top.

With the thread toward the back, hold the tumbler in your left hand and very plainly show the glass, top and bottom. Lift the handkerchief to show the silks in place.

Reach under the handkerchief with your right hand, grasp the knot with your fingertips, and pull down. The yellow silk will pull up over the rim of the glass, under the hankerchief and rubber band, and down the side.

Grasp the silk by the corner and slowly pull it down and apparently through the bottom of the glass.

Remove the handkerchief, show the red silk still in place at the top of the tumbler, and tap the sides and bottom of the glass once more.

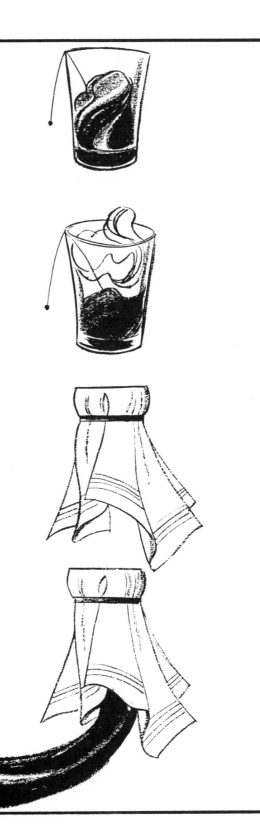

the restored necklace ★★

a neat trick you'll enjoy doing

the effect

The magician shows a pearl necklace. He cuts the string and the beads fall into a waiting glass. He spills the loose beads and string into a small paper bag, waves his magic wand, and when he reaches into the bag, the loose beads and string are once again the lovely necklace he started with.

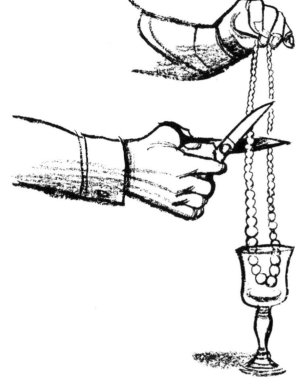

to prepare

Obtain two identical strings of beads—preferably imitation pearls—about twelve inches or so long.

Obtain two small paper bags and prepare them as illustrated.

You will also need a pair of sharp scissors and two wine glasses.

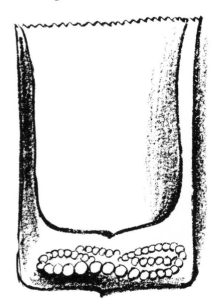

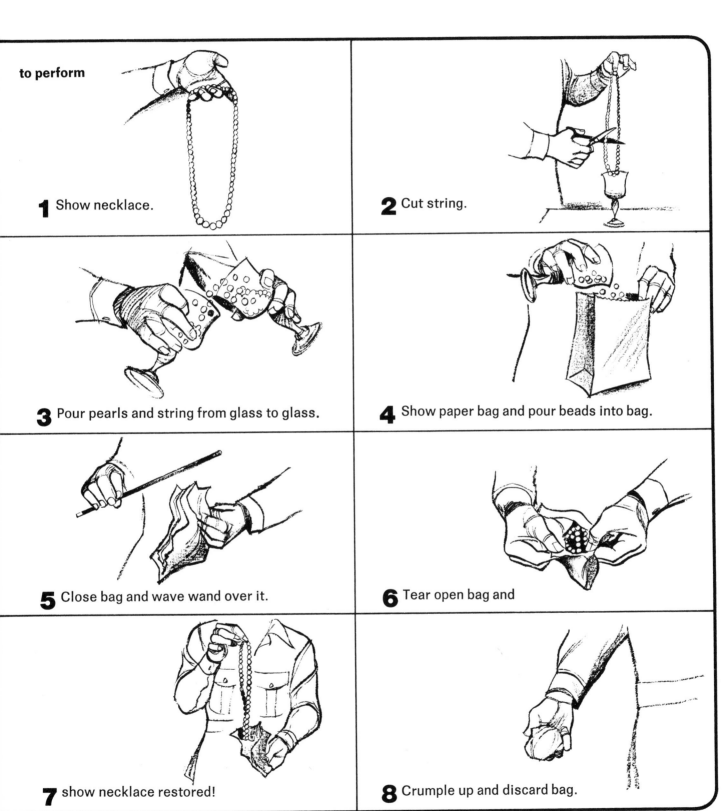

to perform

1 Show necklace.

2 Cut string.

3 Pour pearls and string from glass to glass.

4 Show paper bag and pour beads into bag.

5 Close bag and wave wand over it.

6 Tear open bag and

7 show necklace restored!

8 Crumple up and discard bag.

the stamp-album trick ★★

*an old favorite, and you
can make it yourself*

the effect

The magician flicks the pages of an album to demonstrate that
it is empty. He fashions a cone out of a piece of newspaper
and drops in a handful of stamps. The stamps vanish and
magically appear pasted on the pages of the album.

to prepare

Buy a photo album which is approximately seven
inches high and around twelve inches wide, and
carefully cut every other page ⅛ inch shorter
as indicated.

Paste stamps on every short page, and leave
the alternate pages blank.

Thumb through the pages from one side and the
pages appear blank. Thumb through from the
other and the pages appear full of stamps.

Prepare a utility cornucopia (page 153).

Obtain several hundred canceled stamps.

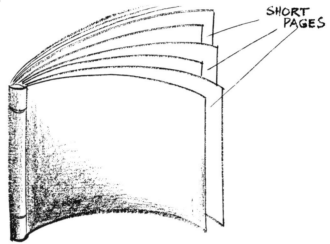

SHORT PAGES

to perform

1 Show a glassine envelope or a clear glass tumbler full of postage stamps.

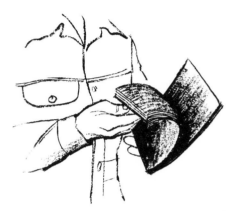

2 Show your stamp album and flick through the pages to clearly show that it is empty.

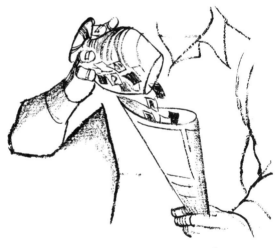

3 Pick up a sheet of newspaper, form it into a cornucopia, and pour in the stamps.

4 Wave your magic wand over the cone and open it up to show that the stamps have vanished.

Pick up your album, flick through the pages, and lo and behold, the missing stamps are neatly pasted into place!

an easy production box ★★

a no-gimmicks, easy-to-make production box

the effect

The magician shows a simple cardboard box unmistakably empty. He reaches in and produces a large load of silks, a live rabbit or anything else he desires.

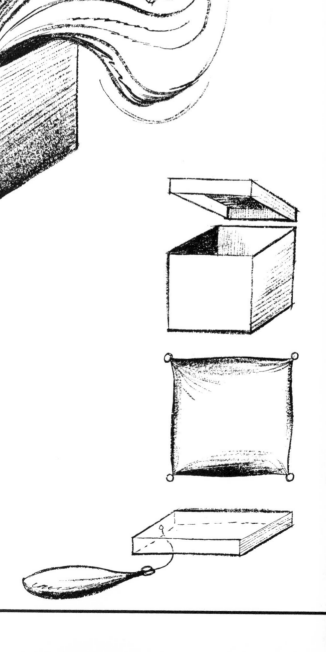

to prepare

Obtain or make a heavy cardboard box and lid approximately ten to twelve inches square.

Paint the inside a light color, cover the outside with Contact paper, aluminum foil or paint, and decorate it to your taste.

Make a production or a rabbit bag as illustrated. Black cloth is generally used, but in this case you would do better to match the color of the inside of your box as closely as possible.

Fold your silks, spring-flowers and/or whatever else you are going to produce, place them in your production bag, and fasten the bag to a small hook that is well secured to the back inside edge of the lid.

If you are just producing silks and flowers you might simply wrap your load in a silk, tie it with weak black cotton thread, and hang it on the lid-hook. To produce, merely break the thread.

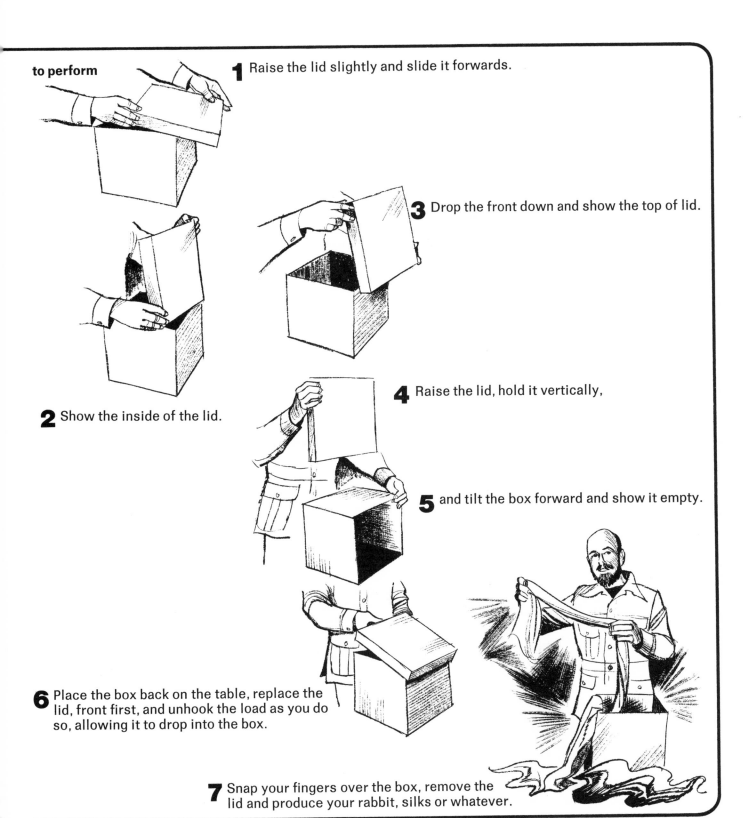

to perform

1 Raise the lid slightly and slide it forwards.

2 Show the inside of the lid.

3 Drop the front down and show the top of lid.

4 Raise the lid, hold it vertically,

5 and tilt the box forward and show it empty.

6 Place the box back on the table, replace the lid, front first, and unhook the load as you do so, allowing it to drop into the box.

7 Snap your fingers over the box, remove the lid and produce your rabbit, silks or whatever.

the penetrating silk ★★

*an ingenious, entertaining
and baffling trick*

the effect

The magician shows a silk, and with a deft motion
causes it to penetrate a solid wooden pole, a
length of rope and any number of other solid
objects.

to prepare

Sew a length of black silk thread to the diagonally
opposite corners of a fifteen-inch silk.

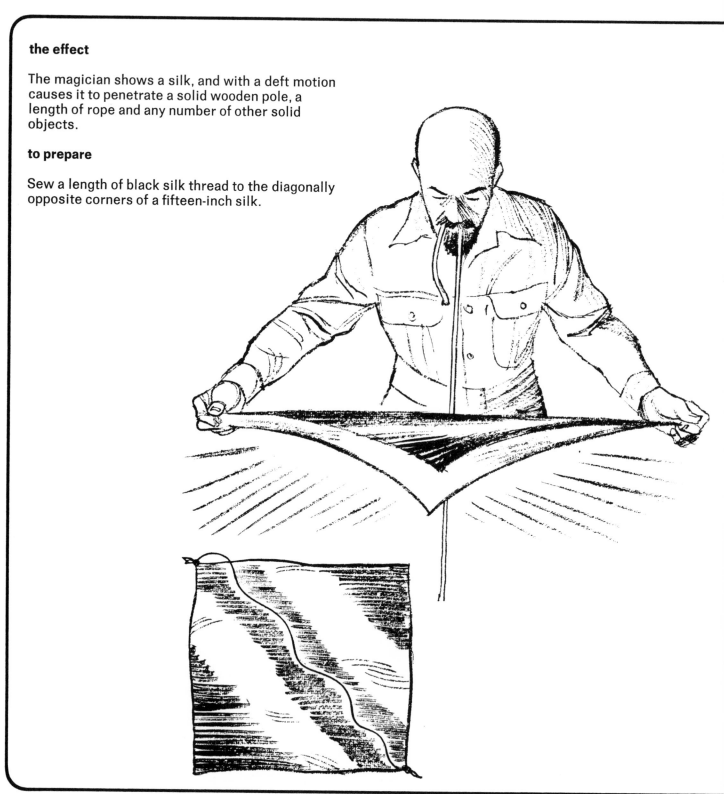

to perform

1 Show a five-foot length of clothesline; snap it between your hands to prove it is solid or have it examined if you like.

2 Drop one end of the rope on the floor, step on it with the ball of one foot, place the other end between your teeth and hold it taut.

3 Place the silk behind the rope, hold as illustrated, and bring ends A and B close together in front of the rope.

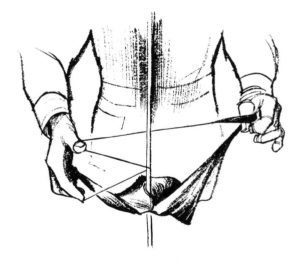

4 Slip your right thumb under the thread, release your hold on corner A, snap the hands apart, and the silk penetrates the rope!

5 Repeat the process to bring the silk back to the other side of the rope.

6 If you prefer not to hold a rope between your teeth, you might have your assistant hold a pole upright against the floor or hold a cane vertically, left hand at the bottom and right at the top.

7 An alternate plan would be to make the silk penetrate the cross-bar of a chair or your leg or your assistant's arm.

8 Practice the move in front of a mirror until you can do it smoothly and well. There are a great many possibilities that will occur to you as you experiment.

continuous
cigarette production ★

self-working, but it looks like pure sleight of hand

the effect

The magician reaches into the air and produces a large number of cigarettes, which he tosses into his hat.

to prepare

Fashion a cigarette-catching gimmick or pick one up at a magic shop.

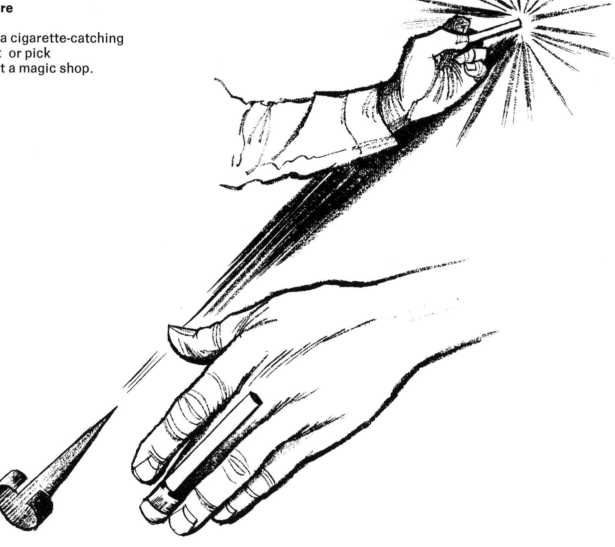

cut from a tin can

File or sand edges smooth and paint flesh-colored.

to perform

Simply reach up, bend your fingers in towards your thumb, and a cigarette magically appears.

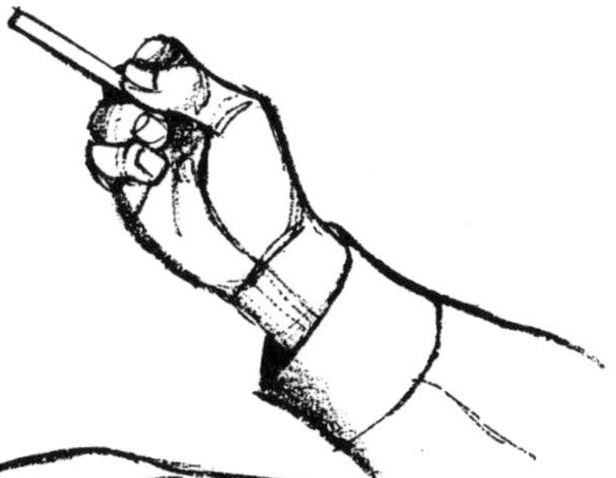

Appear to toss the cigarette into your hat by straightening out your hand, and continue in this fashion. After four or five cigarettes have been produced—more become boring and obvious— turn your hat over and dump out the cigarettes you had secretly placed in it before you began the trick.

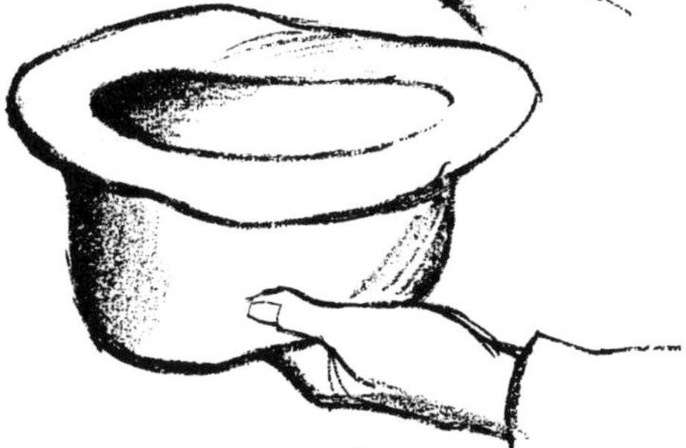

Other objects may be caught in the same way. A similar gimmick could be constructed to catch small balls, provided they are lightweight.

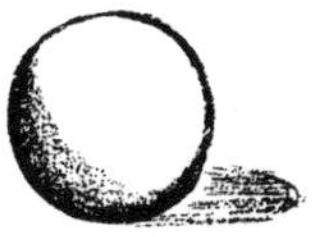

ping-pong ball

ball of crushed aluminum foil

two-hand instant knot ★

a self-working instant knot

Fold your arms and then grasp one end of a length of soft rope in each hand.

Unfold your arms without letting go of the rope, and a knot automatically forms in the center.

snap knot ★

a very perplexing move

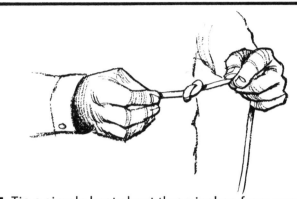

1 Tie a simple knot about three inches from one end of a three-foot length of rope.

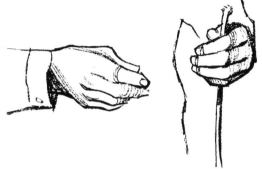

2 Hold the rope between your left thumb and forefinger, the knot hidden by your left palm.

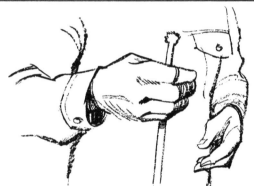

3 Pass the rope to your right hand, holding it in the same position.

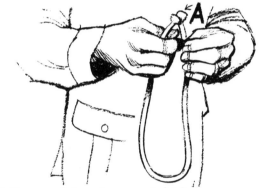

4 Pass end A up to your right fingers.

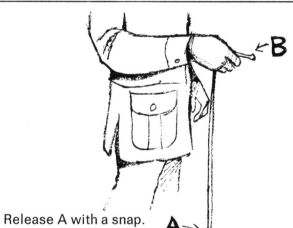

5 Release A with a snap.

6 Repeat.

7 On the third attempt retain A and release end B.

8 You have apparently snapped a knot into the end of the rope!

one-handed knot ★

a quickie knot for use during a rope routine

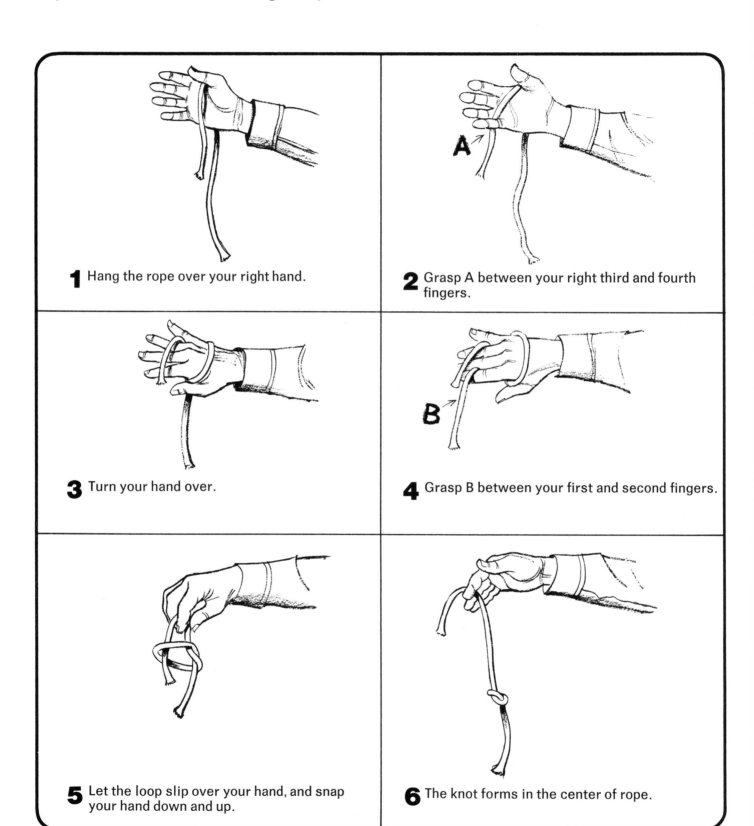

1 Hang the rope over your right hand.

2 Grasp A between your right third and fourth fingers.

3 Turn your hand over.

4 Grasp B between your first and second fingers.

5 Let the loop slip over your hand, and snap your hand down and up.

6 The knot forms in the center of rope.

chalk mark through the table ★

surprisingly effective if it's done well

the effect

A chalk mark penetrates a tabletop and appears on the palm of the magician's previously shown empty hand.

to prepare

Rub as much soft chalk as you can on the fingernail of the third finger of your left hand.

to perform

Place a piece of chalk on the table.

Hold your hands palm upward and show them empty.

Place your left hand under the table and pick up the chalk with your right hand and make a small round dot the size of the dot on your fingernail.

Slowly rub the dot out with the right forefinger as though you were rubbing it through the table.

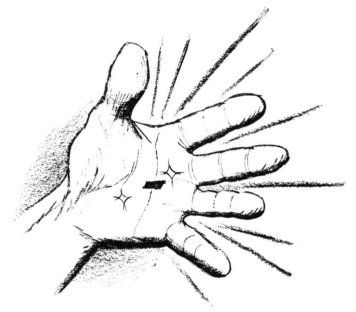

Meanwhile, underneath the table, close your left hand into a tight fist, thus transferring a dot of chalk from your nail onto your palm.

Bring your left hand out from under the table and show that the chalk mark has penetrated the table and is now on your palm.

You will have enough chalk on your fingernail to repeat the trick once or twice more. For your second demonstration you might make the chalk mark penetrate through a door or the bottom of a wooden chair or any other surface that will prevent your audience from seeing you close your fist, which of course would be a giveaway.

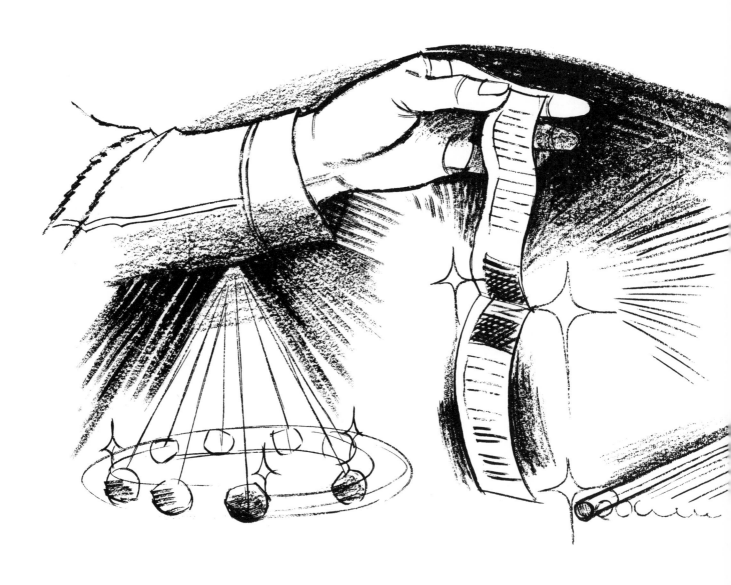

quick tricks

Traditionally magicians have always been
intriguing and often mysterious persons. When
you are able to do magic with almost anything
you touch, you enhance that image—hence the
effects in this section. Admittedly they are far
from earth-shaking, but do them well, at the right
time and under the proper circumstances, and
they can be powerful magic.

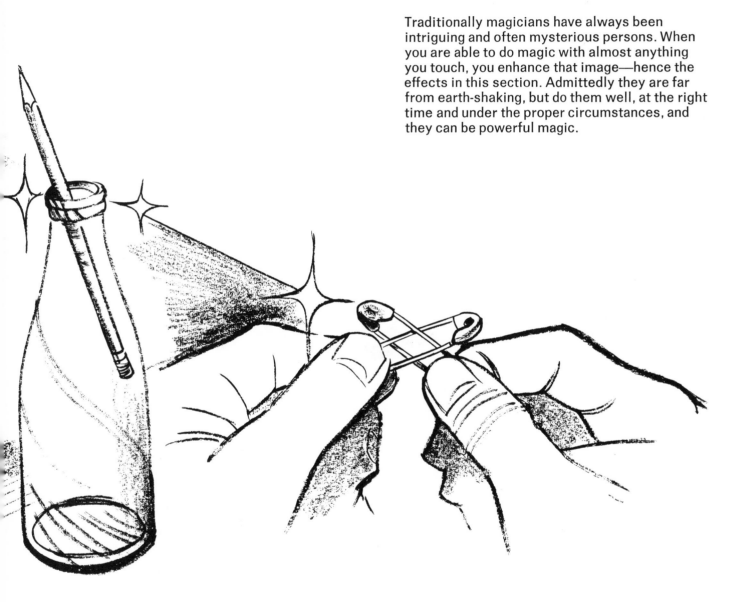

the rising ring ★

Drop an ordinary finger ring over a pencil (or your wand). The ring rises and falls at your command and even answers questions. (One rise means yes, two means no.)

Reverse the wand like this and use the same rig to make the wand rise through your hand.

wood through steel ★

Show an ordinary safety pin to which is attached a short length of dowel stick (or a wooden matchstick). Flick the end of the stick and it penetrates the safety pin.

Actually, of course, the stick goes around the bar, but the illusion is perfect.

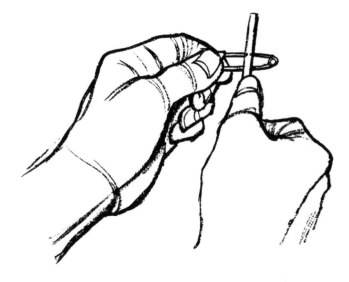

the indestructible handkerchief ★

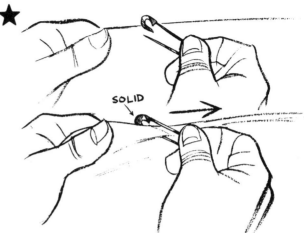

Pin a safety pin securely into a handkerchief or napkin. Grasp the pin firmly and pull it the length of the handkerchief, which, amazingly enough, will remain unharmed!

Hold the pin at an angle and quickly pull parallel with the edge of the handkerchief.

Practice on rags until you acquire the knack.

SOLID

the clinging wand ★

To make your wand or a pencil cling to your hand without visible means of support, place your fingertips exactly as illustrated.

the rising matchbox ★

An ordinary matchbox will rise on the back of your hand if you catch a fold of skin between the drawer and the cover as you close it.

Ralph Read's tapping pencil ★

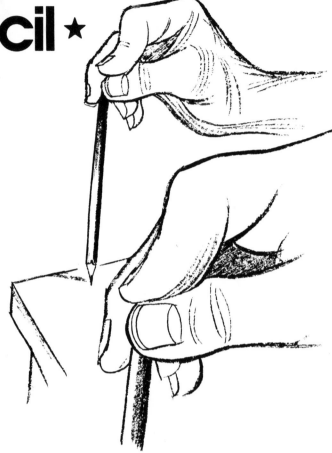

Grasp a lead pencil—the type without an eraser—between the thumb and the first and second fingers, and hold it vertically, the point against the table, as illustrated. Make sure your fingers are dry, and apply as much pressure as you can with your thumb, moving it imperceptibly upwards as you do so, and the pencil will make a series of loud, staccato pops.

This takes a bit of experimentation, but once you get it down, you have a nice little pocket effect that will answer questions and so forth (two taps means yes, one tap means no).

steel through steel ★

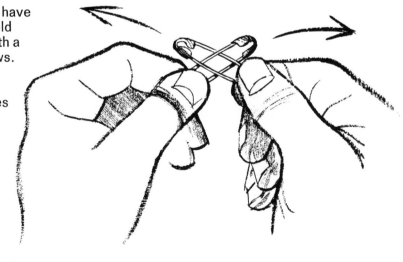

Hand a spectator two large safety pins and have him link them together. Take them back, hold firmly as illustrated and pull them apart with a crisp, hard pull in the direction of the arrows. Apparently steel has penetrated steel.

This takes a bit of a knack. Try it a few times until you get the knack and then it will be quite easy.

the rising match ★

Punch a small, neat round hole in the top of a matchbox and insert a match as illustrated. When the drawer is opened, the match will rise mysteriously.

the diving stone ★

Hang a small, symmetrical stone (or any small weight) on the end of a thin string about fourteen inches long, and explain to your audience that this stone has mystic powers, which, indeed, it seems to! Hold it over a female hand, for example, and it will slowly swing in a circle. Hold it over a male hand, and it will swing in a straight line no matter who is holding it!

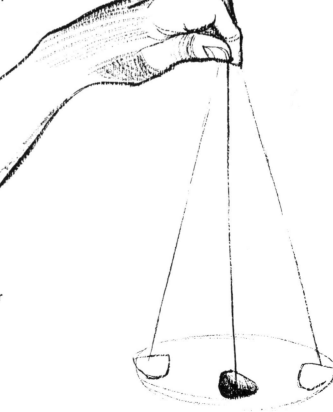

Use it to answer questions as well. Tell your audience that when it swings in a circle the answer is no, and when it swings in a straight line, the answer is yes. It really works.

This is an uncanny effect. Imperceptible muscular activity keeps the stone swinging in a circle or a line despite the holder's best efforts to keep it still. Try it and see.

an easy coin vanish ★

You show a coin in your right hand, openly place it into your left, close your fingers around it, and make it vanish. Both hands are seen to be unmistakably empty.

How? When you pass the coin to your left hand, accidentally drop it. Bend down to pick it up, bring your hand close to your leg, and unhesitatingly, and without looking, drop the coin into your pants cuff. With your hand still clenched as though holding the coin, rise and appear to transfer the coin from your right hand into your left, which closes over it. After an appropriate interval, open your fingers to show that the coin has disappeared.

This is a good move for those moments when you or someone else really does drop a coin.

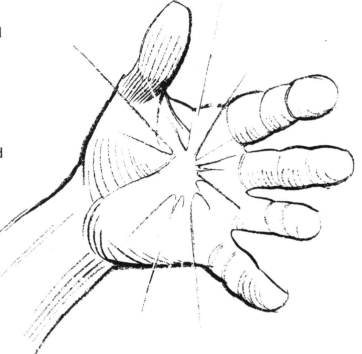

a unique way to reveal a chosen card ★

Take a sliver of fairly soft soap and write the name of a card, say the jack of diamonds (JD), on your forearm. While showing tricks, force the jack of diamonds. Roll up your sleeve, take some cigarette ashes and rub them on your forearm, and "JD" mysteriously appears.

Another possibility . . . Pick up a pad and pencil and openly write the names of everyone present on separate slips of paper. Fold each slip and toss it in a hat. Have someone present select a slip and hold it, unopened. Take a handful of ashes, rub them onto your forearm and the name written on the slip appears.

How? When you wrote the names of the persons in the room on slips of paper, you actually wrote the same name on each slip so that whatever slip was selected would bear the name you had previously written in soap on your forearm.

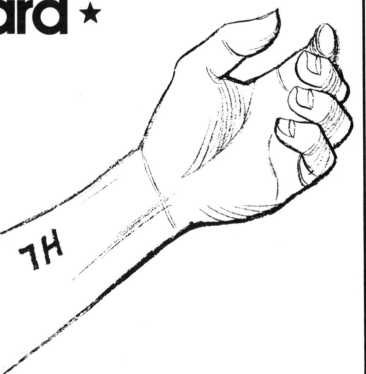

the broken and restored match ⋆

Place a wooden match in the center of your handkerchief, fold the handkerchief over it, and have someone unmistakably break the match. Unfold the handkerchief and the match is restored!

How? You have previously placed a duplicate match in the hem of your handkerchief, and that's the one you have the spectator break.

Work out the moves and do this trick well, and you have a really perplexing close-up effect.

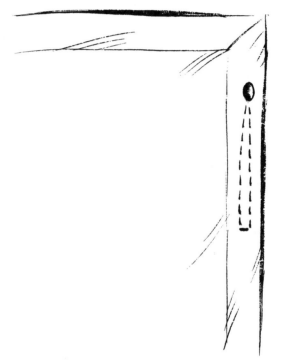

the invisible lasso ⋆

Hold a fairly stiff napkin as illustrated and pantomime lassoing the top of the napkin with a tiny, imaginary lariat. Pull the lariat towards you and the handkerchief bends back just as though a line was really attached to it.

How? Your thumb moves up or down in conjunction with the invisible lariat and that's what moves the napkin. With a little practice you'll soon be able to invisibly move the napkin in almost any direction.

the rolling cigarette ★

Hold a match, toothpick, pen or any similar
object close to a cigarette, and the cigarette
mysteriously rolls away as though propelled by
some strange magnetic force.

How? You secretly (and gently) blow at the
cigarette to propel it.

twin matches ★

Without removing it from the book, tear a match
up the middle. Tear out the match and strike it
just as you would an ordinary match. Then, when
it is lit, peel it into two lit matches.

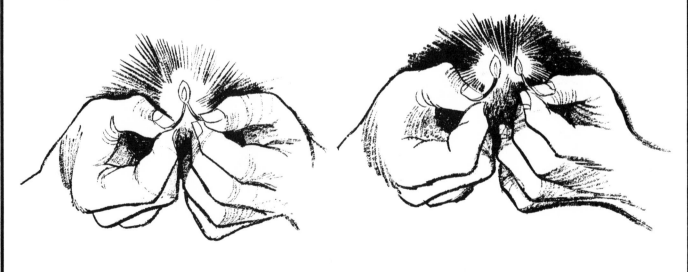

pulse stopping ★

Extend your arm and allow a spectator to feel your pulse. While your wrist is in his grasp, your pulse slows down and finally stops altogether.

Under the proper circumstances this can be powerful magic.

How? You have secretly placed a small ball or a tightly balled handkerchief under your armpit. When you bring your upper arm tightly against your body, the ball presses against the artery, constricting the flow of blood and thus stopping your pulse.

Don't restrict the flow of blood into your arm for more than a few moments at a time.

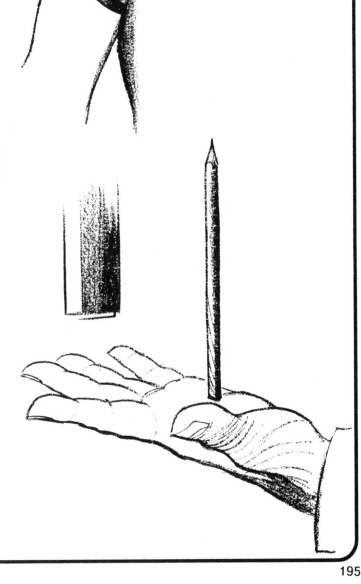

the standing pencil ★

You place what appears to be an ordinary pencil on the palm of your hand, make a mystic pass or two at it, and the pencil slowly rises and stands upright.

How? A pin bent at right angles is attached to the bottom of the pencil. When you place the pencil on your palm you hook the pin into the surface skin of your palm. When your hand is relaxed, the pencil lies down, but when you straighten out your hand, the skin becomes taut and the pencil rises.

On commercially made rising pencils the hook is soldered onto a shell that fits over the end of the pencil. After the pencil rises it may be handed out for examination while the shell remains attached to your palm and thus is unseen by your audience.

195

stunts

Stunts are fun to know and to do. Most magicians know dozens of them. The following have, for one reason or another, intrigued me, so I thought I would pass them along.

clipped ★

This has to be one of the prettiest little stunts ever. Fasten two paper clips on a dollar bill as illustrated.

Grasp the ends of the bill and pull sharply in the direction of the arrows.

The paper clips will shoot three or four feet straight up and come down linked!

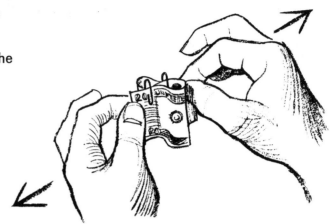

relit ★

If you hold a lit match over a just blown out candle or match, the latter will relight.

How? The flame travels down the smoke.

how to draw
a perfect star ⋆

Cut a strip of paper about half as wide as the star you want to draw.

Carefully tie it into a knot.

Flatten the knot.

Draw a dot at each point in the five-sided figure (decagon) you have made.

Connect the points, and if you have made your knot carefully, you will have drawn a perfect star.

how to float a needle
on a glass of water ⋆

Lay a small piece of fine tissue or cigarette paper on the surface of a small bowl or glass of water.

Carefully lay a needle on the paper.

After a few moments the paper will become waterlogged and sink. The needle, however, will float and continue to for as long as it remains undisturbed.

If you first rub one end of the needle against a magnet it will function as a compass.

the presliced banana ★

Thread a couple of feet of silk thread on a long needle.

Penetrate the banana as illustrated.

Insert the needle back in the same hole from which it emerged, and continue for the length of the banana.

Grasp both ends of the thread, pull firmly, and then remove.

The banana is now sliced in half. To quarter the banana, give it a half twist and repeat the procedure.

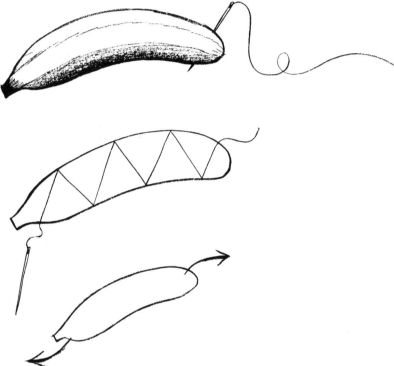

how to empty a bottle faster than anyone else can ★

Hold the bottle upside-down over the sink and rapidly whirl it around in a circular direction. The water is forced to the sides, forming a column in the center through which the air enters as the water rapidly escapes from the sides.

the rising arm trick ⋆

Stand close to a wall, and with your arm stiff, exert as much pressure as you can against the wall. When you pull away from the wall, keep your arm relaxed, and you will feel it slowly rise without any help from you.

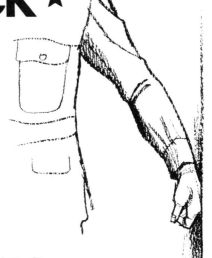

room for one more ⋆

Place a small, dry glass on a perfectly level surface and carefully fill it with water, but be careful not to wet the brim.

Drop a number of straight pins, point first, into the glass and keep going until, believe it or not, the glass contains two or three hundred pins or more, without spilling a drop of water.

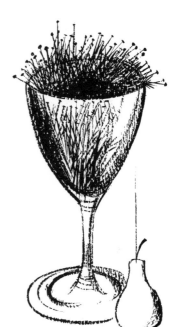

cutting a pear the hard way ⋆

Dip a pear in water, tie a string to its stem and hang it up from an overhead fixture. Note where the drops of water fall and mark the spot. Hold a sharp knife about six inches directly above the water-marked spot, and light the cord with a match. The pear will fall, strike the sharp knife and cut itself in half. (Or quarters if you hold a second knife at right angles to the first!)

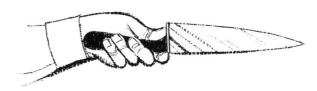

the mouse ★

*in my estimation, the best
of the napkin folds*

the effect

The magician folds a napkin or a clean
handkerchief into a large mouse which, when
properly manipulated, cavorts about as though it
were alive.

to prepare

Obtain a clean napkin or handkerchief—try
various sizes and weights until you find the
right combination for you—and fold as
illustrated.

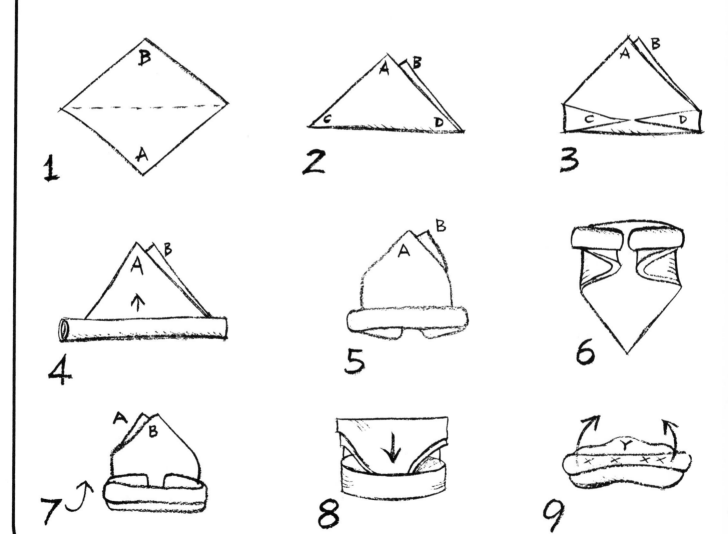

to perform

Cradle the mouse on your left hand, head
uppermost, and as you stroke him with your
right, briskly snap your left fingers toward your
palm. The proper snap will send him scurrying
up your arm. Catch him, repeat, and so on.

Kids love this effect, and believe it or not, one
successful magician has featured it in his
nightclub act for years.

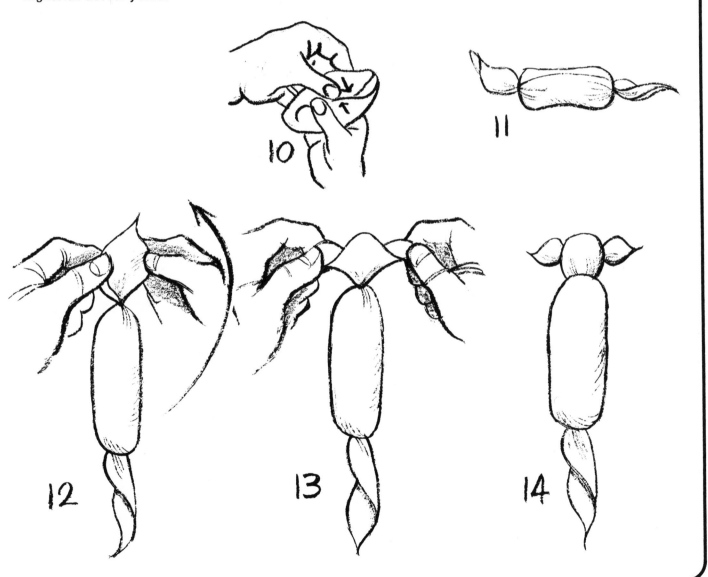

shadography

still entertaining and fun to do

Time was when shadography was a popular form of home entertainment. Like ventriloquism and juggling, it is closely related to magic, and in days gone by, frequently was a part of the program of many magicians. Here, to round out your magical education, are a few of the more popular shadographs.

the elephant
Make the trunk sway and the eye visible.

goat
make him move his head up and down.

the gull
Ruffle the gull's wings and open and close his beak.

the swan
Make the swan turn his head, preen his feathers,
duck his head for fish and rapidly shake his tail.

flying bird
Flap your hands to make the bird fly.

the rabbit
Move the rabbit's ears and legs at the same time.

faces
Make them talk and chew.

the Indian

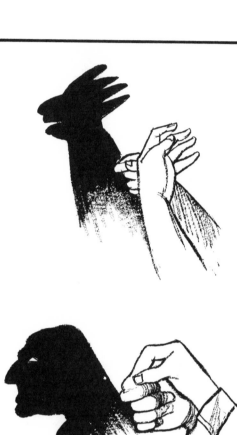

George Washington

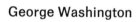

the general

Some performers used simple props—generally
cardboard cutouts of hats and such—to
embellish their figures.

granny

the jockey

Napoleon

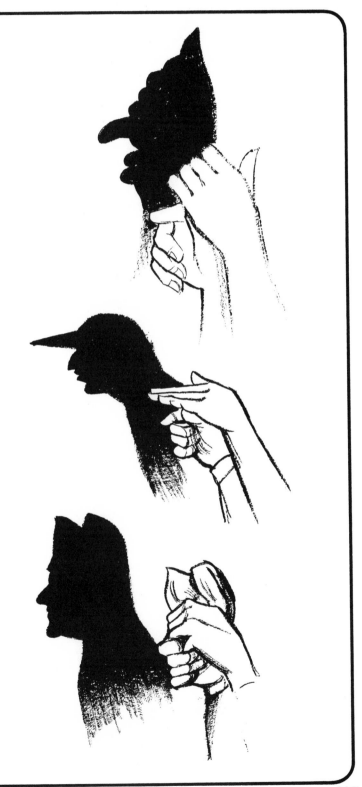

Queen Victoria

the devil

chapeaugraphy

One of the early magic books—a classic work called *The Modern Conjuror and Drawing Room Entertainer* by C. Lang-Neil, which was published around the turn of the century—contains a description of chapeaugraphy and a brief history of it.

The "chapeau" is simply a ring of very heavy felt about seventeen inches across, with a seven- or eight-inch hole in it. You can make your own by laminating four or five layers of regular felt and, to keep it from stretching, binding the edges with matching tape. Size it to fit your head.

It's an extremely versatile device, and all it takes is a few deft twists to transform it into various shapes. Monsieur Trewey, a famous French performer, used it back in the 1880's to present his then-famous "Twenty-five Faces."

Following are some of the more interesting effects as Monsieur Trewey performed them.

the cowboy

No folding. The front rim is turned up, the back pulled down.

the Scotsman

Make a half twist, place on your head and shape as illustrated.

the schoolmaster

Grasp two opposite edges of the ring, draw them about three and a half inches through the center hole, and place the hat on as shown.

the naval officer

Same as the schoolmaster hat, but worn upside-down and with the points fore and aft.

old witch

Twist as for Chinaman, then pass wide end down through the center hole.

the chinaman

Twist twice and place on upside-down.

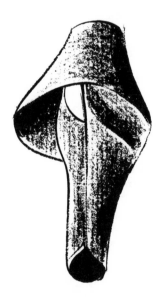

the great magicians past and present

Part of magic's great appeal is its rich tradition and the great men that have helped to make it.

Magicians are almost invariably self-made men. No author writes their lines, no director tells them what to do, no conductor or choreographer guides them through their paces. For the most part, they are highly creative individuals. They write their own material, they invent their own effects, they put together their own acts. Many of them even build their own apparatus.

Most of them have led rich, exciting, adventure-filled lives. Following are a few brief words about some of the more interesting magicians that have—and do—grace stages around the world.

Robert Houdin   French, 1805-1871

Houdin is considered to be the "father of modern conjuring." He was a watchmaker, mechanic, inventor, maker of automatons, an early experimenter with electricity, and the author of several fine books on magic, including his famous memoirs. Houdin became fascinated by magic in his teens after seeing a street conjurer. He traveled with an itinerant magician named Torrini, from whom he learned many basics, and was the first magician to work in a relatively modern manner—that is, in conventional clothes on a relatively bare stage.

Houdin performed before many of the crowned heads of Europe and was greatly renowned and widely imitated. He was one of the first to do a second-sight act in which, by means of a secret code, he conveyed descriptions of objects held by members of the audience to his blindfolded son onstage.

Sent to Algeria by his government to quell a native uprising, he presented magic so impressive the local chiefs gave up their cause as hopeless in view of the superior magic of the French. You'll enjoy reading his memoirs.

Carl Herrmann   German, 1816-1887

Son of an amateur magician-physician, Carl grew up surrounded by magic. Against his parents' wishes he became a conjurer, did his first big-time performance in London in 1848, and quickly became the toast of Europe. He traveled extensively, performed before the crowned heads of Europe, made a fortune and toured North and South America with equal success.

Alexander Herrmann German, 1844–1896 and wife Adelaide

Alexander was Carl's younger brother, his junior by twenty-seven years. When he was ten, he joined Carl and became an adept sleight-of-hand artist. At fifteen he appeared before the queen of Spain. He toured the United States with Carl, and together they met with great success. They separated amicably while in the United States, Carl returning to Europe and Alexander, now known as Herrmann the Great and considered the world's top sleight-of-hand man, staying on in America, where he was a great success.

Herrmann did a spectacular "black art" illusion in which white-clad figures floated mysteriously about a darkened stage, and a great vanishing-lady act that stunned audiences all over America. He married Adelaide in the early seventies. She toured with him and upon his death in 1896 took over the show. In concert with Alexander's nephew Leon, she toured successfully for about a quarter of a century thereafter.

Harry Kellar American, 1849–1922

Harry Kellar ran away from home at the age of twelve, answered an ad placed by an English magician, the Fakir of Ava, and became his assistant. He left the Fakir at eighteen, an accomplished magician and ready to start out on his own. He met with little success, so he joined the famous Davenport brothers as an offstage assistant, mastered their techniques and eventually teamed up with fellow conjurer Professor Fay. After an unsuccessful tour with Professor Fay, Kellar did the vanishing bird cage to great acclaim in Cuba, enjoyed a successful tour through South America, and set sail for Europe with tons of newly acquired apparatus. Shipwrecked near the coast of France, he lost all his equipment and personal belongings. He started fresh, built his reputation and enjoyed several highly successful world tours. He was involved in an intense rivalry with Alexander Herrmann in North America. Upon Herrmann's death, he became the unquestioned leader of American conjurers until 1908, when he retired and turned his show over to Howard Thurston.

Howard Thurston American, 1869–1936

At age seven Thurston saw Herrmann the Great perform, and from that moment on he knew what he wanted to be. Despite a varied career during his youth—he was a newsboy, race-track tout, carnival hanger-on and medical missionary student—he maintained his interest in conjuring and developed into an expert card man.

He made his debut as a six-dollar-a-week circus magician, fooled Leon Herrmann, Alexander's successor-nephew, with his famous rising card trick. Billing himself as the man who fooled the Great Herrmann, he worked his way up through a succession of carnival and dime museums, and eventually became a hit in vaudeville with his specialty, card magic. Dissatisfied, he canceled his lucrative bookings, went to London and built a full evening show that was an instant hit. After an artistically triumphant, financially dismal world tour he joined Kellar, toured with him for a year, and then became his successor. At one point Thurston had over thirty assistants and over thirty tons of apparatus in what was surely the largest, most lavish and spectacular show of its kind ever. He died at the age of sixty-six, the most famous illusionist of them all.

Chung Ling Soo (William Robinson) American, 1868–1918

An inventor and builder of illusions and an assistant to magicians, including Harry Kellar, he became Alexander Herrmann's stage manager and did Herrmann's act when the master was indisposed. After several attempts to perform on his own with little success, he made up as a Chinese, patterned his act after the then famous Ching Ling Foo, and became an instant success. He performed productions of tubs of water with ducks swimming about and other feats of an Oriental nature. When challenged by the former, he managed to convince the world that he, not Ching Ling Foo, was the genuine Chinese. One night his feature trick, in which expert marksmen fired bullets that he caught on a china plate, failed, and Chung Ling Soo fell dead onstage, a victim of the dangerous bullet-catching trick.

Harry Houdini American, 1874–1926

Born Ehrich Weiss, of a desperately poor immigrant family, he learned his first magic trick at fourteen, was professional at seventeen, and got married at nineteen. His wife Bess joined the act, and after six years of abject failure he made a moderate success with handcuff escapes. He went to London and escaped from Scotland Yard's strongest handcuffs. The resulting publicity stimulated bookings, and Houdini was on his way. He made ever more daring escapes. He was lashed to a loaded cannon with a twenty-minute fuse and escaped in thirteen. Tied to a track fifteen minutes before a train was due, he barely escaped as the train screamed by. He escaped from filled milk cans, packing crates, ropes, chains and every conceivable constraint, and smashed box office records doing it.

Houdini was an early pilot, was first to fly an airplane in Australia, and was the first to make adventure-movie serials in which he made hairbreadth escapes without doubles. In love with magic, he became the president of the Society of American Magicians, wrote books on the subject, visited the graves of magicians all over the world, collected enormous quantities of magic memorabilia and exposed fraudulent spiritualists wherever he could find them.

Houdini was backstage when a student asked if it was true he could withstand pain, but before he could answer he was struck in the stomach. He refused to quit working, and in seven days, on Halloween evening, he died of a ruptured appendix.

T. Nelson Downs   American, 1867–1938

T. Nelson Downs, known as the King of Koins, was one of the most highly paid and most widely imitated magicians in vaudeville. He was a master coin manipulator, a specialist in the back and front palm with coins, and famous for his spectacular Miser's Dream, a trick in which he produced showers of coins from the air.

Max Malini   American

Max Malini was a legendary character who performed in the early years of this century. He was a celebrated close-up worker who despite his lack of education and his unimpressive appearance was a society favorite and a frequent performer before many of the crowned heads of Europe.

Nate Leipzig   American, 1873–1939

Old-timers still speak with awe of Nate Leipzig's card-handling. His delightful personality, his superb presentation and his brilliant card-handling made him a great vaudeville favorite, despite the fact that he worked large theaters with no more than a deck of cards rather than a stage full of complex apparatus.

Harry Blackstone   American, 1885–1965

Harry Blackstone was the last of the great full-evening illusionists. A master showman, at one point in his career he traveled with a troupe of twenty-six performers and assistants and seventy tons of apparatus, but despite the excellence with which he presented his big illusions, it was his handling of small magic—particularly his Haunted Handkerchief—that really entranced audiences. His death in 1965 ended an era.

Cardini Welsh, 1894–1973

A celebrated performer whose twelve-minute act was, in the opinion of many (including this writer), the most beautiful in magic and one of the most widely imitated. A dazzling sleight-of-hand man and a superb all-around magician, Cardini's specialties were the production and manipulation of cards, cigarettes and sometimes billiard balls. He worked in pantomime and would enter meticulously dressed in top hat and tails and wearing white gloves and a magnificent purple-lined cape. To his surprise, beautiful fans of cards appeared at his fingertips in seemingly endless profusion. Lit cigarettes popped out of nowhere, and sometimes huge varicolored billiard balls as well. Cardini's act was an artistic triumph. To have missed it is to have missed a great magical experience.

Slydini American, 1900–1989

Slydini was perhaps the magician's favorite magician. He was a great innovator whose unique style and close-up magic technique were very influential.

the contemporaries

It is an almost impossible task to single out contemporary performers for special mention. There are so many brilliant magicians gracing the current scene—for example,

Dai Vernon, one of the world's great sleight-of-hand men, a great artist and brilliant innovator, has spent his entire life (he is in his nineties now, and he started at the age of five) furthering the art of magic, and not for fame or fortune but for the sheer love of it. . .

Frank Garcia, the man with the "million-dollar hands," whose grace and dexterity with cards, coins and billiard balls is almost beyond belief, and whose delightful sense of humor and superb presentation is equal to his great skill . . .

Larry Jennings, one of the favorite magicians of magicians, a great sleight-of-hand man whose brilliant innovations and close-up magic technique have enthralled the magic world for years . . .

Shimada, young Japanese magician who produces doves and silks and Japanese parasols in such endless profusion and with such consummate skill that even magicians are awed and impressed . . .

Siegfried and **Roy,** who present the most spectacular, action-packed magical extravaganzas ever . . .

Darwin Ortiz and **Derek Dingle,** who are so incredibly skilled with a deck of cards that they have become legends in their own time . . .

David Copperfield, the brilliant young magician and illusionist whose uncanny effects, superb presentation and total dedication to magic make him the outstanding magician of this era, and probably of all time . . .

Coin manipulator **David Roth,** who has older, more experienced magicians shaking their heads in disbelief . . . **Harry Blackstone, Jr.,** who performs illusions with uncanny grace and ease . . . **Max Maven,** who does one of the cleverest acts in mental magic, and on and on . . .

These and many, many more have achieved a degree of skill almost undreamed of by so many magicians of bygone eras.

Someday, if you are really interested, who knows? Perhaps your name will be added to the list.

books of special interest

Magicians are prolific book writers. There are thousands of books and manuscripts on every aspect of magic. Some are so elementary they are really of no practical value. Others are so highly technical only specialists with a great degree of expertise can even begin to understand them. Many, however, are good, solid books ideally suited for anyone interested in magic, including those of you who have only recently become involved.

Greater Magic by John Northern Hilliard

An encyclopedic work—over 1,000 pages of mostly good magic. The emphasis is on cards, but there are sections on balls, silks, cigarettes, coins, sponge balls and so forth, and there are lots of tricks you can do with simple props you can scrounge up around the house. A good reference work too.

Modern Coin Magic by J. B. Bobo (His grandfather spelled it Beauxbeaux!)

Written in the forties, this book is already considered *the* classic work on coins, and deservedly so! It tells you everything you should know about every aspect of the subject, and contains enough fine sleights and superb tricks and routines, many contributed by top magicians, to keep you busy for a lifetime. If coins are your passion, Bobo is a must. [Dover reprint]

The Tarbell Course by Harlan Tarbell

The original course was put out long years ago. Since then, it has been added to, revised, gone through a great many editions and several different publishers, and is still going strong! There are seven volumes in the set, and together they comprise a complete and very good course in magic.

The Illustrated History of Magic by Milbourne Christopher

A fascinating history of magic and magicians written by one of our foremost conjurers and magical historians. If you are going to be involved in magic, you certainly will be intrigued by its grand traditions and the fascinating people who were its stars and superstars. This lavishly illustrated book tells you a great deal about them. I enjoyed it thoroughly, and I am sure you will too. [Dover has *Magic: A Picture History* by this author]

The Memoirs of Robert Houdin

The still fascinating memoirs of the nineteenth-century French magician many consider to be the father of modern conjuring. Watch and automaton maker, inventor, dabbler in electricity, and the most successful magician of his era, Houdin's story is a must for any lover of magic.

Houdini's Escapes and Magic by Walter Gibson

This is a fairly old book (originally published over forty years ago), and there isn't really too much material that you can personally use to advantage unless you are contemplating the Chinese water torture escape or have aspirations to walk through brick walls, but it does make fascinating reading and present a keen insight into the art—and science—of magic, particularly escapes and illusions. Walter Gibson, one of our foremost and most prolific writer-scholars on the magic arts, presents this and everything he does in highly readable and enjoyable fashion.

Encyclopedia of Card Tricks by Jean Hugard

The late Jean Hugard was perhaps the foremost writer of magic books for magicians. Generally thin paperbacks, virtually devoid of illustrations, and not too highly detailed, they are nevertheless authoritative and all-inclusive. His books cover the gamut— thimbles, silks, dinner-table magic and especially cards. His encyclopedia is a superb collection over four hundred pages long, and is certainly worth having if card magic intrigues you. [Dover reprint]

Abbott's Encyclopedia of Rope Tricks for Magicians, compiled by Stewart James

This classic work contains over one hundred and fifty effects with rope—enough material to keep anyone interested in this branch of the art busy for a lifetime. Most of the good rope tricks appear here—cut and restoreds, penetrations of various types, tricky knots, ties and so on. This is an interesting book and a good one for your library. [Dover reprint]

Scarne on Card Tricks

John Scarne, who is probably the world's leading authority on gambling techniques and games, is also one of the most highly regarded card and close-up workers. In this book, he has assembled over one hundred and fifty card tricks, many of them first-rate effects you will enjoy doing.

glossary

Apparatus The visible equipment magicians use in the performance of their tricks.

Acquitment A sleight in which a palmed object is secretly passed from hand to hand so as to make the hands appear to be empty.

Assistant A magician's helper who is part of his entourage and appears with him during his act.

Back Palm A palming technique in which the objects—generally a card(s) or coin(s)—is concealed behind the fingers of either hand.

Bit A fragment of a sleight or magical effect.

Break A slight opening secretly held in a deck of cards.

Change The magical transformation of one object into another.

Color Change A sleight which changes the color of an object.

Confederate A secret assistant who appears to be an ordinary spectator and whose relationship to the magician is thus unknown.

Conjurer A magician.

Disappear An act by which a formerly visible object is rendered nonexistent.

Discovery The revelation of a playing card whose identity was unknown to the magician.

Effect A sleight or trick.

Finger Palm A palming technique in which the object is concealed behind the partially closed fingers of either hand.

Force A technique in which the selection of an object—generally a card—is forced on a spectator who is under the impression that he is making a free choice.

Flash Paper Tissue paper treated with nitric acid that flares into flame upon contact with a glowing cigarette or lit match.

Gimmick A secret device used in the execution of a magic trick.

Glimpse To secretly note the suit and denomination of a card.

Illusion A stage effect using large apparatus.

Legerdemain A French term for magic of the hands or sleight of hand.

Load An object or group of objects concealed on the person (or elsewhere) and ready to be stolen for subsequent production or use; the act of secretly introducing an object into another location.

Location The act of secretly locating a particular card in the deck.

Magician A performer of magic tricks or illusions.

Marked Cards A deck of cards secretly marked so as to enable the magician to read the suit and denomination from the back.

Misdirection A technique or maneuver by which the magician directs the audience's attention away from that which he does not want them to see and/or towards something he does.

Move A sleight or portion of a sleight.

Palm To secrete from view by hiding in the palm of the hand, behind the fingers, at the root of the thumb, behind the hand or someplace else on the hand.

Pass A sleight.

Patter The talk a magician uses to accompany a trick.

Penetration The magical passing of one solid object through another.

Prestidigitation A French term for magic or sleight of hand performed by a prestidigitator or magician.

Produce To make an object or objects that were formerly nonexistent suddenly appear.

Production A trick in which objects are produced from an empty receptacle (rabbit from the hat) or from the air (cards, fans).

Riffle The noise and motion created when the magician

depresses the corner of a deck of cards with his thumb and suddenly releases it.

Routine A flow or sequence of sleights or effects which blend into a smooth, harmonious act or segment of an act.

Shell A hollow half-object, such as a ball, shell or a hollowed-out backless coin, in which a smaller coin may be concealed.

Shuffle The process of mixing a deck of cards.

Silk A colorful square of very thin compressible cloth, formerly China silk, now generally nylon, ranging in size from 12 inches by 12 inches to 36 inches by 36 inches.

Steal To secretly gain possession of an object, generally from somewhere on your person.

Stripper Deck A gimmicked deck in which all the cards have been trimmed to a wedge shape, thus enabling the magician to locate a card by having it replaced into the deck in reverse position.

Sucker Move or Trick A move or a trick or segment of a trick especially planned to give the audience the impression that it knows how the trick is being done.

Switch A sleight or move in which one object is secretly substituted for another.

Talk The telltale sound an object makes when it accidentally strikes against another during the course of a trick.

Trick A deception in which the audience is fooled.

Vanish The act of making an object suddenly become nonexistent.

Volunteer A temporary helper drafted from the audience and used by the magician to aid in the consummation of the trick.

About the Author

Like a great many magicians, Bill Tarr, author of *Now You See It, Now You Don't: Lessons in Sleight of Hand* and *The Second Now You See It, Now You Don't: More Lessons in Sleight of Hand*, has been interested in magic from a very early age. He did his first tricks at the age of nine, spent the greater part of his youth with a deck of cards in his hands, and eventually did a manipulative act—cards, billiard balls and cigarettes—professionally . . . a brief interlude he most thoroughly enjoyed. After a hitch in the Navy he entered the arts, and for many years has been a dedicated full-time sculptor.

He is a former Guggenheim Fellow, a Municipal Art Society Award winner, and creator of several of America's largest sculptures, including the Martin Luther King, Jr., Memorial, the huge Morningside Heights piece and some twelve other works in New York City alone.

Husband of prominent cookbook author Yvonne Young Tarr, and father of two sons, Jonathon and Nicolas, he works and lives in East Hampton, New York.